Reflective Practice for Social Workers

Reflective Practice for Social Workers

A Handbook for Developing Professional Confidence

Linda Bruce

 Open University Press

Open University Press
McGraw-Hill Education
McGraw-Hill House
Shoppenhangers Road
Maidenhead
Berkshire
England
SL6 2QL

email: enquiries@openup.co.uk
world wide web: www.openup.co.uk

and Two Penn Plaza, New York, NY 10121-2289, USA

First published 2013

A catalogue record of this book is available from the British Library

ISBN-13: 978-0-335-24408-9
ISBN-10: 0-335-24408-4
eISBN: 978-0-335-24409-6

Library of Congress Cataloging-in-Publication Data
CIP data applied for

Typeset by Aptara, Inc.

Fictitious names of companies, products, people, characters and/or data that may be used herein (in case studies or in examples) are not intended to represent any real individual, company, product or event.

Praise for this Book

"This is a well-written text that provides much-needed clarity around a central process within professional social work. Students, practitioners and managers will learn lots about how to use reflection effectively. Linda Bruce writes with authority and a deep understanding - she has done an excellent job."

Steve Hothersall,
Head of Social Work Education, Edge Hill University

"This is an extremely important area of practice in the current complex world of social work practice and social care. This book takes students and practitioners through the relevant knowledge and theory base and appropriate tools for reflection. I thoroughly recommend it."

Joyce Lishman,
Professor Emeritus, Robert Gordon University,
Aberdeen

For Bill and Kim

Contents

Acknowledgements

I would like to thank the social work students, academic and practice colleagues and service user and carer participation groups I have worked with for their contribution to my own reflective journey, which made this book possible.

Thank you to the Institute for Research and Innovation in Social Services (IRISS) and the Oxford Centre for Staff Learning and Development for their kind permission to reproduce material within the book, and to Katherine, Abigail and numerous 'critical' friends for their ongoing encouragement and support from conception to completion.

Note to the reader:

On 31st July 2012, during the completion of this book, the professional regulatory body, the General Social Care Council (GSCC), referred to in the text, was abolished. On 1st August 2012 the Health and Care Professions Council (HCPC) assumed responsibility for the regulation and registration of social workers in England, as a result of the Health and Social Care Act 2012. Social workers in England will be required to meet HCPC standards of proficiency, conduct, performance and ethics relevant to their area of practice and comply with standards for continuing professional development (CPD). Details of the HCPC's role and function can be found at www.hcpc-uk.org.

1   Introduction

If you're browsing through this text it suggests you are looking for a resource that will help you grasp the concept and application of 'reflective practice'. This action in itself is a positive indicator of your ability to take responsibility for your own development, a crucial first step to becoming a reflective practitioner.

This text aims to provide one key resource that will demystify the reflective process and offer an accessible and practical approach to developing your knowledge, understanding and application of reflection in practice.

Reflective practice has a central role to play in the ongoing professional development of the social work workforce and as a result is incorporated in all aspects of social work education and training – from initial qualifying programmes to post-qualifying awards. The content of this text is pertinent to those experiencing their first encounter with the concept, to those revisiting the subject as a result of ongoing education and training opportunities, and to practitioners who have supervisory responsibilities for social workers in training during practice learning experiences. To capture the wide range of students who will be expected to evidence reflective practice as part of their education or training programme, the text will collectively refer to 'learners' throughout the content, unless discussing an area that has relevance for only one group, such as 'social workers in training'.

The content included in this text has been accumulated and developed over a number of years as a result of my responsibility for the design and delivery of the teaching and learning curriculum for this subject on both initial qualifying and post-qualifying social work education programmes.

In the role of lecturer, tutor or mentor I have found the subject of 'reflective practice' to be an area that most learners have consistently found challenging. As a result, I have been afforded the opportunity to gather a range of useful learning resources that have enabled previous learners to effectively develop their understanding of reflective practice and become more confident in the application of their reflective skills. The purpose of this text, therefore, is to share these tried and tested resources more widely in the hope that it will help others to develop their competence and confidence as reflective practitioners. My thanks go to the many learners who have contributed to these developing teaching and learning approaches.

Social work practice is a complex task and qualified practitioners have wide-ranging professional responsibilities in many vulnerable people's lives. Professional registration requires practitioners to continually engage in ongoing professional development through post-qualifying training and scholarly activity, creating a professional culture that recognizes the value of continuous learning throughout one's professional career.

Those joining the profession face a rigorous education and training programme designed to enable them to develop the professional knowledge, skills and values that will equip them to become competent in the roles and responsibilities they will undertake as newly qualified social workers. A feature of this rigorous training is the requirement to evidence the development of multiple professional standards and overall professional competence within a set time frame. It is not unusual for social workers in training to be focused on the assessment process, seeing the successful achievement of each assessed task as the goal required to progress through each stage of their course. For many, the integration of theory with practice can prove challenging and practice learning placements play a central role in facilitating progress in this area. 'Reflection', however, does not sit comfortably alongside functional requirements and standards as it requires each individual to accept and engage in a developmental process that acknowledges their uniqueness, their stage of learning, their style of learning, and their ability to self-assess. The fluidity of this process can feel at odds with the desire to develop strategies for 'how to' successfully produce concrete evidence of skill development or professional knowledge for academic or practice learning assessment tasks.

All social workers in training will be introduced to the concept of reflective practice during their initial professional education and training as a result of the widespread acknowledgement given to its place in the development of a confident and competent workforce. How or when you are introduced to the concept of reflection will vary across social work programmes, but it is likely that you will be expected to evidence reflective practice during practice learning experiences and be asked to produce examples of reflective writing as evidence of your development in this area.

It is understandable that all learners will focus on those areas that are influential to a successful outcome, but in my experience the developmental processes that form part of professional development – such as reflection – are not always highlighted explicitly, and therefore can be overlooked until a task requires it. This leaves little time for a learner to understand the concept or master the practice which results in a loss of confidence in their reflective abilities and leaves a potential gap in the evidence required to achieve the standards necessary in professional education. This book aims to highlight the clear link between the development of reflective practice and the successful completion of the functional aspects of professional competence. It should enable you to see a purpose to the process of reflection and the potential for enhancing the subject evidence produced for others, such as academic staff or practice teachers/educators. By 'normalizing' the concept of the reflective practitioner, it can become embedded in your development as a professional and become an activity that will directly influence the development of your professional confidence and competence. Encouraging you to invest in the reflective process early in your studies will allow you the space and time to develop your knowledge and skills in this area, in preparation for events such as practice learning experiences or entering the workforce at the point of qualifying.

This book aims to provide you with one core text that will provide all the components necessary to develop a good working knowledge and understanding of reflection and reflective practice. The content sets the 'reflective practitioner' at the heart of the confident and competent professional, and argues that such a practitioner will provide a more effective service to those who use social work services, and their carers.

Initially you are invited to give some thought to what it means to be a 'professional', acknowledging the responsibilities that come with such status in society. A summary of the key theoretical concepts that underpin our understanding of reflection will be provided, and you will be afforded the opportunity to enhance your ability to relate to others by developing your knowledge and understanding of *emotional intelligence*. You will also be provided with a range of tools that can be used to aid the reflective process and will be encouraged and enabled to develop the skill of reflective writing. Learning in practice is central to the development of professional competence and confidence as it provides invaluable opportunities to learn from 'real-life' experiences. To ensure these opportunities can enhance growth and development, the creation of a positive learning environment that is conducive to reflecting 'in' and 'on' practice is explored, alongside the key features that ensure competent assessment of student performance in practice. The concept of reflexivity is offered, an addition to the practitioner's reflective toolbox, as an approach to enhance self-evaluations undertaken by those practitioners who have responsibility to facilitate the learning of others.

Overall, the structure of the text will encourage you to be an active participant by offering opportunities to engage in activities that will allow you to record your thoughts and learning as you develop your reflective knowledge and skills. The completion of these activities will add depth to your learning and are therefore recommended.

The following summaries of each chapter's content are provided to help you effectively navigate your way through the text and focus on your own learning needs.

The focus of Chapter 2 will be to consider the personal responsibilities and external expectations associated with professional status. The concepts of 'profession' and 'professional' will be discussed, and you are invited to consider how these apply to the roles and responsibilities social work has in society today. The 'crisis in confidence' experienced by many professionals will be explored, and the resulting role played by reflective practice in addressing this 'crisis' will be highlighted. The standards for professional performance required by government and the public play a crucial part in the quality of existing service delivery, so the concept of 'professional performance' is discussed in conjunction with significant key features such as professional knowledge, values, and a commitment to ongoing professional development. Some explanation is provided for what constitutes professional knowledge, and the contribution of evidence-based practice to the credibility of this knowledge base is acknowledged. Consideration is given to the role of professional ethics and values in creating a shared sense of professional identity, with specific attention being given to the importance of the application of the General Social Care Council (GSCC) and Scottish Social Services Council (SSSC) codes of practice in guiding practice decisions and providing a statement of professional standards for all. A commitment to ongoing professional development is highlighted in social work's code of ethics and code of practice, as well as a requirement in all aspects of professional education and training. This requires each individual practitioner to engage in activities that will result in the maintenance and improvement of professional performance. This chapter will explore the meaning of professional development and argue that the skill of reflective practice is central to learning from experience and that it underpins the ongoing development of professional confidence and competence.

The journey to becoming a social work professional will be contextualized by making links to the requirements and standards currently identified for social workers in training, drawing briefly on:

- national occupational standards
- standards in social work education
- professional codes of practice
- the 21st Century Review of Social Work (Scotland), and
- the outcomes of the Social Work Taskforce and Reform Board (England).

The role that professional education has in the development of a confident and competent workforce will be discussed, and the activity of reflection, lifelong learning and continuous professional development will be encouraged as a means of ensuring a competent workforce for the future.

Many individuals incorporate a degree of reflection in their personal lives, but for professional performance and development this potentially natural activity requires an enhanced level of knowledge and understanding of the process if you are to ensure that experiential learning can bring about positive change in your practice. Chapter 3 will provide you with a summary of a range of theoretical perspectives that underpin our understanding of the concept of reflection and reflective practice today. A historical context will be provided through an outline of the classical work of John Dewey, Donald Schön and David Boud, followed by a summary of the perspectives of some contemporary writers such as Jennifer Moon, Jan Fook, Neil Thomson and Gillie Bolton.

By capturing this knowledge base in one section you will have the opportunity to see the development of the concept over time and consider how it can be applicable to social work practice today. Having the theoretical perspectives summarized will provide you with an easily accessible knowledge base to aid understanding of the concept and highlight the similarities and differences in each of the approaches discussed. This chapter can also act as a reference source, as required, over time, or as a revision source for practitioners who are looking to revisit their knowledge and understanding of reflection.

In Chapter 4 you are encouraged to consider the relevance of emotional intelligence for social work practice and explore the significant role that reflective practice can play in enabling you to develop the key features of intrapersonal and interpersonal competence that will enhance your ability to relate to others. Emotional intelligence relies on your ability to develop emotional self-awareness and understanding so that you can appropriately manage your emotional responses in practice and become more effective at recognizing, acknowledging and responding to the emotions of others. Your capacity to become emotionally self-aware determines the levels of emotional intelligence you can achieve, and for this reason the chapter also includes an outline of cognitive learning theory as a source of knowledge that can be utilized in the reflective process to enhance the development of emotional awareness and understanding.

Becoming a reflective practitioner relies on your ability and willingness to apply the knowledge, understanding and skills you have achieved and to find a way to ensure reflection becomes an integral part of your practice routines. In Chapter 5 you will be provided with a brief insight into the common obstacles experienced by those who have struggled to achieve reflective practice, with practical suggestions offered that can ensure you avoid these same obstacles impacting on your own reflective practice. This chapter will also introduce a range of reflective tools that are intended to encourage learners to engage with the reflective process by providing practical, structured, activities that allow you to experience the application of the theory outlined in Chapter 3 and facilitate the development of your reflective skills. These reflective tools will introduce you to a range of reflective questions that aim to stimulate your thinking and encourage the analysis of your experiences. The structure provided by these accessible tools will prove useful when gathering evidence of your developing reflective skills, both for your own use, but also as evidence for others who may be involved in an assessment process. The tools described will also encourage you to draw on all the component parts of reflection – i.e. professional knowledge, skills, values and emotions – allowing you to consider how each component enhances the reflective process.

Having considered a range of reflective questions and become familiar with the available tools that facilitate the reflective process, Chapter 6 will focus on the development of reflective writing skills that will effectively document the internalized conversations encouraged by the reflective process, for yourself and others.

Reflective writing plays a significant part in learners' professional development as it increases the quality and depth of learning achieved from retrospectively critically examining practice experiences. These written reflective accounts capture current thinking, awareness and knowledge, create an ongoing record of professional progress, and provide evidence of professional competence to others.

This chapter will consider the purpose, challenges and benefits of reflective writing and offer practical guidance on 'what' and 'how' to write reflectively to enable you to establish or consolidate your competence and confidence in this valuable professional skill.

The discussion in Chapter 7 is centred around the crucial feature of learning in practice and is written specifically for social workers in training and those responsible for supervising part or all of the practice-based elements of students' professional education and training. The opportunity to learn in practice is crucial to the development of professional competence and confidence, but the depth of learning achieved, and the reliability of assessment outcomes, are determined by features within the workplace environment.

The chapter will focus on the creation of a positive learning environment, identifying and exploring four key elements that enable and encourage reflection 'in' and 'on' practice and ensure an accurate account of students' achievements and professional development is captured in the assessment process. The elements being explored include developing learning partnerships, redefining power relations, the adult learning experience and effective supervision, each making their own crucial contribution to the creation of an environment that is conducive to learning from practice experiences and facilitating professional development. The assessment of students' performance is a central feature of practice learning experiences, but the accuracy and reliability of the assessment outcomes are enhanced when the assessment process becomes an integral part of existing learning partnerships. The purpose, processes and principles that guide competent assessments are outlined to establish a shared understanding of this central feature of practice-based elements of professional education and encourage active participation from all key participants. The final section of the chapter will explore the concept of reflexivity and consider its value for practitioners and supervisors committed to monitoring and evaluating the quality of their own performance.

The final chapter, Chapter 8, will reinforce key messages from previous chapters in order to capture the knowledge, understanding and skills you have available to inform your development as a reflective practitioner and enable you to confidently move forward and take responsibility for the quality of your future practice and professional development.

I take for granted that you are an individual with a strong sense of social justice, a desire to make a positive difference in people's lives, and motivated to provide a high-quality professional service to others. I hope that the content provides you with a new perspective and understanding of reflective practice, a new sense of confidence in your developing knowledge and skills, and a clear focus for how to make full use of reflection to aid your future development.

2   Becoming a professional

The process of becoming a professional, and sustaining professional standards of practice throughout your social work career, is at the heart of ensuring the provision of
high-quality services to those individuals who may need care, support or protection in
our society. While external organizations exist to regulate and monitor the quality of
professional education and service provision, it is the responsibility of each individual
practitioner and social worker in training to achieve and sustain professional standards
of practice, with institutions such as universities and social service employers having a
responsibility to provide opportunities and support to enable you to achieve this goal.

The reason for choosing this topic as a starting point for the book was twofold. Firstly,
from a very practical point of view it seems obvious that the longer you have to think
about what is required to achieve and sustain professional standards, and the more time
you give yourself to put into practice what you have discovered, the more comfortable and
confident you will become. Secondly, from a developmental point of view, it is important
to acquire a clear grasp of the 'bigger picture' of what it is you are working towards – your
eye on the final goal of becoming a 'competent and confident professional' (Scottish
Executive, 2005). By understanding what is required and expected of a professional social
worker you will be in a stronger position to take control of the pace and direction of your
own learning and development, which in itself is an important professional attribute.

By the end of this chapter I hope you will have developed a greater awareness of
what it means to be part of a profession and have a new understanding of the central
role that reflective practice plays in the provision of a professional service and your ability to sustain an acceptable level of professionalism in your working practice over time.

To begin this process it seems appropriate to set the scene by including a brief
historical perspective of the development of the professional role and society's expectations of service provision from those who have professional status, before going on
to consider our own journey as a social work profession. These events provided a back-
drop to current policy and practice and have been influential in shaping current professional education and training and contemporary professional practice, including
social work.

Professionals and society

During the 1970s, society made increasing demands on a wide range of professional
services which led to practitioners feeling overwhelmed and at times unable to manage
the issues that were being presented. The 1980s were a time of societal change, when

consumerism grew in strength and government sought 'value for money' through the provision of public services that were efficient and effective. During this time an unprecedented range of errors in professional judgement, inconsistent standards of practice, and misuse of professional autonomy were reported, resulting in the public losing faith in professional expertise and values and calling for governments to create systems to regulate and monitor professional practice. The public were questioning the credibility and adequacy of professional, expert, knowledge, and professionals were seen as ill-equipped to deal with the problems society was experiencing. Rather than fulfilling their claim to contribute to society's well-being, professionals were seen as ignoring their obligation to public services and inadequately policing themselves.

During this time many professions were self-critical of their own failures and questioned the adequacy of their professional knowledge to deal with the tasks they were required to perform. Schön captured the mood when he wrote 'professional knowledge is mismatched to the changing character of the situation of practice' (1983: 14). This loss of confidence in professional knowledge, by the public and professionals themselves, also led to questions being asked about the quality of professional education and discussion on how to develop new approaches to education and training that focused on developing 'competent' professionals who were able to meet societal needs and restore public and professional confidence.

By the 1990s, professions – particularly those providing public services – were under closer scrutiny, experiencing increased government financial control and more regulation, monitoring and evaluation. Performance indicators and target setting were introduced by governments across much of Europe as a means of identifying, measuring and controlling service provision, creating an easily accessible structure for formal inspection and public reporting. During the development of performance indicators the occupational roles performed by many professions were analysed so that decisions could be made about the standard of service the public could expect. Occupational functions were outlined and specific criteria for standards of practice were identified. Having this ability to measure a profession's performance against set criteria was thought to serve the political aspirations of being able to provide the public with evidence of a competent workforce, working efficiently and effectively to provide quality services, thereby rebuilding public confidence in the professional workforce. Operationally, organizations providing professional services developed systems that would enable them to provide evidence that targets had been met and occupational standards achieved. This practice resulted in the workforce experiencing increased levels of bureaucracy, proceduralization, and a more managerial approach became dominant in the workplace. For practitioners, this change was extremely challenging as they saw the increase in recording and form filling, the development of instructions for what they must do when, and the necessity to be focused on meeting set targets as undermining their role as autonomous practitioners and at times this resulted in action that conflicted with their professional values. These circumstances resulted in professionals feeling that they were no longer trusted to use their discretion, design services to meet individuals' need, and apply professional knowledge and values in practice.

Educational institutions also experienced stricter regulation, and new competency-based professional programmes designed around occupational functions and standards of practice were introduced with new regulatory bodies created to approve, monitor and regulate professional education and training programmes.

The implementation of these changes in many of society's key professional institutions involved consultation with relevant professionals and academics in an attempt to identify an appropriate way forward. This was seen by the research community as an opportunity to contribute, and positively influence, this process of change. There was a great deal of debate in the international literature of the time that focused on finding a definition of 'a *profession*' and 'a *professional*', with the intention of providing a clear statement of agreed qualities and characteristics that society could expect of these occupational groups, in the hope that public confidence could be restored, government standards could be maintained, and the integrity and complexity of professional practice could be recognized and valued.

Defining 'profession' and 'professional'

Despite the significant interest and debates in academic literature to define the concepts of '*profession/professional*' it proved difficult for international researchers to initially reach a consensus due to the broad nature of occupations that held professional status and the lack of comparable translation in European languages.

Arguably, one of the most cited definitions of '*profession*' came from the work of Burrage, Jarausch and Siegrist (1990). Their early definition of 'a *profession*' argued that these groups consisted of 'full-time, non-manual workers' who had 'a monopoly in the labour market for expert services' which were provided by occupations that had achieved a level of 'self governance'. Practitioners required a qualification, which involved intellectually challenging, 'scholarly' activity, before being allowed to enter these occupations. As an occupational group they were seen to experience job satisfaction that was the result of having a shared set of occupational values and competence and a belief that their role was important in society (1990: 205).

Sociologist David Sciulli (2007) reiterated many of the views highlighted almost two decades earlier, but also added to the arguments by stating that the qualifying training provided for *professions* should have a theoretical and analytical basis that encouraged mental activity and was rigorously assessed. He argued that *professions* would have established occupational standards and practices that were informed by relevant knowledge, analysis, reflection and evaluation and would provide a range of services that were transparent to the wider public and open to feedback.

We have some general agreement in the literature that *professionals* should make a positive contribution to the well-being of our society (Schön, 1983; Burrage et al., 1990; Jones and Joss, 1995) by providing competent services, carried out by practitioners who are knowledgeable (Eraut, 1994; Jones and Joss, 1995; Thompson, 2000) and are committed to continuously improving their performance by ongoing learning (Walker, 1992; Eraut, 1994).

Siegrist (2002) offered a definition of '*professional*' that argued for basic essential characteristics – such as having a knowledge that was 'exclusive', not easily understood by a layperson, and been achieved through education. The professional should have 'rules and attitudes' informing the application of this knowledge and 'an orientation towards the common good' (cited in Sciulli, 2005: 921). Sciulli highlighted the power imbalance between professionals and service users, arguing that professionals 'occupy an entrenched position of power, trust and discretion' and, as a direct result of this, those who use professional services will 'occupy entrenched positions of dependence, vulnerability and apprehension' (2007: 143). However, he believed that as a profession 'matured', it became apparent that the occupational standards applied in practice actively attempted to empower service users, but acknowledged that the power differential would 'never disappear entirely' (2007: 144). Initially, when Sciulli highlighted the power imbalance in professional–client relationships he argued that *professionals* had a responsibility to enhance the well-being of individuals and the communities in which they were based. In his view, if *professionals* were to function for the common good, he believed they had a responsibility to continually evaluate the appropriateness and currency of their knowledge base and adapt services to the changing needs of the individuals and communities they serve (Sciulli, 2005).

Competence and professional performance

Since the 1990s, academic literature has highlighted concern that an explanation of 'competence', based purely on occupational functions and set performance indicators, was regarded as overly simplistic and did not reflect the complexity of the situations professionals functioned within, or sufficiently captured what was involved in professional practice. In an attempt to provide a more informed, and arguably accurate, account of professional practice, researchers focused their attention on how best to define professional performance.

While acknowledging that different professions perform different functions, some common key features of professional practice were identified in subsequent literature. An example of some of the consensus reached at the time was summarized by Jones and Joss, (cited in Yelloly and Henkel, 1995) who identified four key themes as significant features of professional performance:

- working with uncertainty
- theoretical knowledge informing practice
- the application of professional values, and
- the approach taken to professional development.

Dealing with uncertainty and finding solutions to match individuals' unique situations was regarded as a familiar scenario for professionals, requiring a variety of differing approaches and an ability to use their discretion when choosing appropriate action. For practitioners to manage this aspect of practice it was believed to be a 'professional responsibility to continuously improve personal performance' (Jones and Joss, 1995: 21).

The acquisition and maintenance of a theoretical knowledge base that would inform practice decisions had also been previously accepted as one of the necessary characteristics of a professional.

The role of occupational values was seen as significant to professional performance, not only in how it influenced the professional–client relationship, but also how it influenced the development of professional identity and worth in its members, shaping a professional culture.

A profession's chosen method of how best to facilitate the professional development of its members was believed to be a 'significant determinant of professional performance' (Jones and Joss, 1995: 22).

Having identified these significant professional performance features, Jones and Joss argued that there was a range of potential models of professionalism. One such model that had emerged in response to 'external pressure' (1995: 23), but also encapsulates the pertinent qualities and characteristics previously highlighted by earlier research, was the model of 'The Reflective Practitioner'. In this model:

> 'The role of the professional's self-image is one of facilitator whose role is to help find an optimal course of action or solution to problems in an uncertain world.... The relationship with the client is at the centre of professional practice. It is a collaborative on-going dialogue which is facilitated by, but not controlled by, the professional.... Professional development occurs through a process of experiential learning from doing. Learning is through analysis, by observing, reflecting, experimenting and conceptualizing... and involves responsibility for continuous professional growth and development.'
>
> (Jones and Joss, 1995: 26)

Reflective practice had long since been regarded as a process that facilitated professional development as it allowed practitioners to 'return to their experiences and draw out new understandings' (Boud et al., 1985: 19), which was crucial given the complexity and uniqueness of the situations professionals encountered in their daily practice. Reflective practice offered a means to consider what is informing practice by checking the adequacy and currency of our knowledge, quality of our skills, and the influence of personal values to each unique interaction so that we could apply this learning to future practice, thereby ensuring we continually develop as practitioners.

This brief look at the literature offers some insight into the development of current professional standards of practice expected by society and governments. It also clearly establishes a professional's own responsibility to ensure competent practice through ongoing professional development and continuous learning.

In summary, we have identified that becoming a professional involves:

- Achieving an educational qualification that provides a range of theoretical, research-based, professional knowledge and is intellectually challenging.
- Being able to provide 'competent' services that are informed by occupational standards.
- Taking responsibility to continually evaluate the appropriateness and currency of one's knowledge base and adapt practice accordingly.
- Being committed to a shared set of occupational values that underpin the approach to practice.

- Being committed to continuously improving one's performance through ongoing learning.
- Making a positive contribution to the well-being of individuals and communities.

Further exploration of the concept of 'competence' offers a clearer understanding of the professional performance expected within a professional role and includes:

- An ability to deal with uncertainty.
- An ability to apply a range and breadth of knowledge to our understanding of each unique situation and identify appropriate solutions to fit individual needs.
- An ability to use one's own discretion when making decisions.
- An ability to apply professional values to work undertaken.
- A commitment to ongoing professional development.

Activity

Having considered briefly how research has informed our understanding of the concepts of 'profession' and 'professional', how does this fit with your own thoughts?
   Take a few moments to record your own views:

- Describe your image of a professional.
- What qualities and characteristics do you associate with 'professionals'?
- Which of these attributes do you already possess?
- Which of these would you like to acquire and which would you like to avoid?

Having considered the qualities and features that the literature suggests define a professional, we can apply this insight to help us understand the process that has shaped the development of social work as a profession.

The profession of social work

Before considering social work in the twenty-first century it seems appropriate to contextualize the very early development of the 'caring' profession, highlighting the clear influence that public opinion, social problems and political and economic agendas have had in shaping service provision and recognizing the continuous process of change the profession has experienced over time. A more detailed account of social work's history can be found in Cree (2011), Horner (2009), Payne (2005) and Jones (2002).

Social work, as we know it, began to emerge in the nineteenth century as a direct response to social problems created as a result of the industrial revolution. This period shows an increasing number of public institutions emerging to manage the social problems being experienced by society – problems directly attributed to poverty and the breakdown of family structures due to labour migration. Legislation was emerging which allowed the state to implement change, such as compulsory education for children, power to detain individuals with mental health problems or learning disabilities in institutions, and the removal of children from their home if parents failed to provide adequate care. As society experienced an increase in legislation and social control, government required a profession that could enforce the legislation, and large numbers of social workers were employed by state agencies to carry out this role.

In parallel, an increasing number of charitable, voluntary (philanthropic) organizations were also emerging, particularly to provide services for children, driven by key middle-class reformers such as Dr Barnardo, Elizabeth Fry and Florence Nightingale. These early practitioners had a clear function and purpose which resulted in the formation of The Charity Organization Society (COS) in 1869. The COS approach was informed by a belief that individuals had the ability to take responsibility for personal change in their circumstances and saw casework as a means of addressing social problems and influencing social reform (Jones, 2002, cited in Horner, 2009).

Cree (2011) offers a useful observation of our history at this time, identifying the 'care' and 'control' functions that both the state and charitable organizations operated over those who received services, and within services, through strict rules and eligibility criteria.

The eradication of poverty was the key focus for service delivery in the early twentieth century with the voluntary and statutory residential and fieldwork services existing in parallel, providing services for children, offenders, older people, those with disabilities and some community work. As the state established greater social control through legislation the relationship between the statutory and voluntary service providers experienced significant change as 'statutory agencies also became responsible for regulating and controlling the voluntary sector, through funding and inspection arrangements' (Cree, 2008: 296).

The creation of the welfare state brought the next period of major legislative and policy change affecting the profession in the United Kingdom. Key services such as social security, education, the National Health Service and housing departments were formed as part of the plan to reconstruct British society after the end of the Second World War, with social work being afforded the task of 'picking up the small number of people who might fall through the welfare net and rehabilitate them so that they could again play their part as full citizens' (Cree, 2008: 296). The voluntary and private sector continued to provide a diverse range of services to those who fell outside of the statutory services responsibility.

In an attempt to create effective services to families the government established a committee, chaired by Sir Frederick Seebohm, 'to review the organization and responsibilities of the local authority personal social services' (Seebohm, 1968). The Seebohm Committee recommended that local authority social service departments should deliver 'universal and integrated services' to all those in need, based on the principle that individuals would only require 'one door on which to knock' (Seebohm, 1968). To ensure quality generic services could be provided, the committee also recommended the establishment of a generic education and training programme for qualified social workers – the Certificate of Qualification in Social Work (CQSW) – approved and regulated through a statutory professional body known as the Central Council for Education and Training of Social Workers (CCETSW), which was established in 1971. The recommendations of the Seebohm Committee led to the Social Work (Scotland) Act 1968 and the Local Authority Social Services Act 1970 (England and Wales).

The introduction of this legislation resulted in social work being firmly located in local government functions, 'offering an integrated service from the cradle to the grave' (Horner, 2009: 92) and identifying the role of the voluntary sector as one that would 'supplement local authority work' and as a 'stimulus to further progress' (Social Work (Scotland) Act 1968). The new professional qualification (the CQSW), introduced in 1972, aimed to provide society with social work practitioners who were capable of fulfilling a generic role that could facilitate change within families and communities as a result of their shared professional knowledge, skills and values.

The 1980s and 1990s saw the Conservative Government's New Right Policy advocate that the state should not be responsible for the provision of all social welfare needs, and introduce compulsory competitive tendering, which brought the beginning of the mixed economy of care. With these new initiatives came a managerial approach to service delivery, driven by quality assurance systems, target setting, performance indicators and external inspections, to satisfy the new culture of consumerism and government efficiency measures.

In 1989 a new, competency-based, professional education and training programme was introduced. It was designed around the outcome of a functional analysis of the social work role, identifying the knowledge, skills and values required for the next generation of newly qualified social workers. Given the complexity of the social work role, greater emphasis was given to the need for practitioners to develop skills in analysis, evaluation and reflective practice. The development of reflective skills was regarded as a prerequisite for effective social work practice (Horner, 2004) as it provided opportunities to 'learn from our experiences and enhances our knowledge and skills' (Knott and Scragg, 2007: 49), thereby informing our ongoing professional development. CCETSW maintained their regulatory role at this time, approving courses and monitoring standards across the United Kingdom.

British society became dissatisfied with the Conservative Government's New Right policies, and in turn became dissatisfied with the standard of public services, including social work. Under the New Right policies, society had experienced restricted access to social work services, and an increasing number of those in need of care were required to make a financial contribution for it. Statutory social work services were limited to focusing on those individuals requiring protection, control, or who were at risk, without means or alternative support.

In 1997, with the election of a New Labour Government, the next major change for social work was initiated through the *Modernising Social Services* White Paper (Department of Health, 1998) and the *Building for the Future* White Paper (Department of Health, 1999). A parallel process was occurring in Scotland, initiated by the *Scottish Modernising Social Work Services: A Consultation Paper on Workforce Regulation and Education* (Scottish Executive, 1998), and in early 1999 the Scottish White Paper with proposals for the modernization of Scottish social work services, *Aiming for Excellence: Modernising Social Services in Scotland* (Scottish Executive, 1999). These initiatives were a direct response to the public's concern about inconsistent service standards across the United Kingdom, a lack of access to, and availability of, appropriate services, and a lack of inter-agency collaboration. Horner summarized the purpose of the Modernizing Social Services White Paper (1998) as 'intending to reform the strategic direction of social work, create structures for social work regulation, and focus on modernizing social services and improving the status of, and the public's confidence in, the social work profession' (2009: 116), a purpose mirrored in the Scottish debate. A useful critique of New Labour's 'Third Way', highlighting the need for critical practice in social work, is provided in Paul Stepney's article 'Mission Impossible? Critical Practice in Social Work', published in the *British Journal of Social Work* (2006) 36, 1289–307, accessible at www.bjsw.oxfordjournals.org

The 'modernization' agenda was to be realized through the reorganization of social work services, creating 'new shared ways of delivering services that are individually tailored, accessible and more joined up' (Department of Health, 2000). Service users, and their carers, were seen to be crucial partners in the new arrangements developing across health and social care, the private and voluntary sectors, and within local authority departments such as social work and housing. Service delivery packages conveyed the interdependency that had developed between statutory and voluntary service providers as voluntary organizations relied heavily on local or central government funding and statutory services relied heavily on the wide range of support services offered by the voluntary sector (Cree, 2008). The newly created partnership arrangements also introduced greater multi-agency collaboration and required social workers to develop a clear sense of the unique contribution they would make to service delivery in this new environment. This required social workers to be confident in their own professional identity, recognizing the value of the professional knowledge, skills and values they brought to the inter-professional table.

The United Kingdom experienced constitutional change during this time as a result of the successful devolution process for Scotland, Wales and Northern Ireland. Since 1999, the Scottish Parliament has had the power to create legislation affecting key services, including social work. In the same year the National Assembly for Wales came into force (but without legislative powers), and in 2007 the Northern Ireland Assembly was created, with the facility to engage in the development of legislation affecting social work services.

A significant national outcome of the Labour Government's 'modernizing of social services' consultation was the introduction of legislation that created new independent regulatory bodies and, for the first time, a process of professional registration for qualified social workers and protection of the title of 'social worker' in the United Kingdom.

The Care Standards Act 2000 was introduced to reform the regulatory systems for care services in England and Wales, and the National Care Standards Commission (NCSC) was established. This was subsequently replaced by the Care Standards Inspectorate for Wales (in 2002), and followed by the establishment of the Regulation and Quality Improvement Authority (RQIA) in Northern Ireland (2005) and the Care Quality Commission (CQC) in England (2009). These new independent regulatory bodies are charged with the responsibility to register and inspect care services against a set of national care standards to ensure service quality and standards are maintained.

The Care Standards Act 2000 abolished the CCETSW and replaced it with new independent bodies: the General Social Care Council (GSCC) in England, accountable to the Secretary of State; the Cyngor Gofal Cymru/Care Council for Wales, accountable to the National Assembly of Wales; the Northern Ireland Social Care Council (NISCC), accountable to the Northern Ireland Assembly. These regulatory bodies were responsible for the regulation and registration of social work practitioners and the approval and regulation of social work education and training programmes. The new councils were commissioned to develop a code of conduct for the profession as a means of raising standards in practice, and to facilitate and maintain a register of all suitably qualified social workers.

In Scotland, an identical process was occurring though the implementation of the Regulation of Care (Scotland) Act 2001. This established the Scottish Commission for the Regulation of Care (SCRC) as the regulatory body that would register and inspect care services against agreed national care standards, and the Scottish Social Services Council (SSSC), accountable to the Scottish Parliament, to regulate and register social work practitioners and to approve, regulate and promote social work education and training.

Both pieces of legislation make it illegal for anyone who does not hold an approved social work qualification to identify themselves as a 'social worker', thereby protecting the title and practice of social workers from misrepresentation. Further information on regulation, inspection and the registration of social workers can be found on the local regulatory body and professional councils' websites. See Appendix 1 for contact details.

A further, but equally significant, change that occurred as a result of the 'modernizing' agenda was the decision that social work should become a graduate profession, in line with other professional occupations. A new honours degree programme was introduced in England in 2003, with the rest of the United Kingdom following in 2004. The content of the new qualification is designed around the Quality Assurance Agency for Higher Education (QAA) Benchmark Statements (QAA, 2000) that describe the knowledge, skills and values expected of a newly qualified practitioner, and a common set of national occupational standards (NOS) (Training Organization for the Personal Social Services (TOPPS), 2002). The NOS were the result of an occupational functional analysis, undertaken in consultation with service users, informal carers, social work employers and social work practitioners, to identify the roles and responsibilities of twenty-first-century social workers. The GSCC codes of practice (2002a) are embedded in the NOS. The code of practice is shared by the profession across the UK, and the NOS have minor inter-country variations, such as the order of the identified key social work roles. Full local details can be found on each of the professional councils' websites, but the key roles are provided for you in Appendix 2.

The new *Requirements for Social Work Training* (Department of Health, 2002) and the *Framework for Social Work Education in Scotland* (SSSC, 2003) outline, for social work education providers across the UK, the selection, teaching, learning and assessment requirements that should be embedded in their programmes to ensure adequate opportunities are available for each social worker in training to achieve competence in the required key roles, knowledge and skills before entering the profession. In Scotland, the learning requirements for all social workers in training – identified in the Framework for Social Work Education in Scotland (SSSC, 2003) – are captured in the Standards in Social Work Education (SiSWE), which incorporates the NOS key roles, the QAA benchmark statements and the GSCC (2002a) codes of practice. In 2006, the Scottish Executive also required all social workers in training in Scotland to demonstrate 'key capabilities in child care and protection', by the point of qualifying, to ensure all newly qualified practitioners were competent to identify and respond to the needs of children at risk or in need of care (Scottish Executive, 2006).

Each local professional council has the responsibility to approve, monitor and regulate higher education establishments offering a social work programme in their area to ensure standards are maintained. Each social worker in training is required to register with the appropriate professional council in their local area, and therefore comply with professional registration requirements, from the beginning of their professional career.

The new social work education programmes are designed to:

> improve service standards by producing social workers who are: competent to work across a wide range of settings; confident in what they know and can do; clear about their professional identity and that of other professionals; flexible and adaptable; committed to continuous improvement; responsive to change in a positive way and able to contribute to the development of the profession.
>
> (SSSC, 2003)

To help social workers in training achieve these professional outcomes the new professional programmes were structured to ensure that students would spend time in both academic study and practice learning. This aimed to ensure that social workers in training could develop their skills, confidence and competence in applying professional knowledge and skills in direct practice situations. The new programme also required social workers in training to develop their knowledge and understanding of the needs and experiences of both service users and their carers. This initiative was to lead to service users and informal carers actively participating in the delivery of social work education programmes in recognition of their 'expertise', and in keeping with the new partnership arrangements occurring in practice.

This summary, outlining social work's evolution, highlights how each of these historical events brought new challenges for the profession. There have been many occasions when these challenges raised questions about our professional survival, our professional worth, or our ability to maintain the integrity of our professional values. Arguably it is the strength of our commitment and motivation to enable those individuals who are marginalized and vulnerable in our society that has been a constant driver behind our efforts to successfully manage the challenges that we are presented with. Social work is an activity that is built around change, and professionally we have had to cope with the associated loss of 'old ways' and find opportunities to develop and grow (Marris, 1974). Social work is a moral activity (SSSC, 2003) as well as a political activity (Drakeford, 2008) and we have to manage the tension between our legal responsibilities and duties, as outlined by the state, and our commitment to the principles of client-centred practice and individualization, as outlined by our professional values and codes of practice (GSCC, 2002a, 2002b; SSSC, 2005). This tension has been a constant challenge to social work since the beginning of the welfare state, and will remain a challenge for us in the future. The social work role continues to be a complex activity, where dealing with uncertainty is a normal component of practice but at odds with the political, organizational and societal need for concrete systems that measure and evidence performance. While this tension continues to bring the profession many challenges it is crucial that we actively resist any attempt to reduce social work practice to merely carrying out a list of set tasks or focusing on outcomes. 'We must not allow the deprofessionalizing tendencies of managerialism and consumerism to reduce us to bureaucrats with professional accountability reduced to following orders' (Thompson, 2009: 199) as 'the realities of practice are far too complex to rely safely on direct instructions, habits or formula responses' (Thompson and Thompson, 2008a: 12).

What is important about our contact with service users is the way we go about the task, how we do it, and the significant part our interpersonal relationships play in facilitating a service user's ability to change (Trotter, 1999). In building this relationship a social worker's 'use of self' is a key resource and crucial influence in the service user's experience. So in many respects the profession's future rests within the profession itself, and requires all of us to commit to continually developing the depth and range of the professional knowledge and skills that inform our practice, being guided by our professional values and embedding critically reflective practice into our routines. If we achieve this, then we can maintain a competent and confident professional workforce that has a unique contribution to make to the well-being of society in the twenty-first century.

The social work profession in the twenty-first century

If we return to the definitions of '*professionals*' outlined earlier in the chapter we can see that social work's claim to professional status in the twenty-first century is supported by the existence of an intellectually challenging professional qualification prior to entering the profession, a set of agreed practice standards and shared set of professional values, and a registered and regulated workforce.

The society and political landscape in which we function and serve are, however, consistently changing, and as a result we as a profession need to adapt and change accordingly.

In Scotland the *Changing Lives* report (Scottish Executive, 2006) presented the way forward for twenty-first-century social work with recommendations that included a clear role and purpose for social workers, the responsibilities of social service employers to support a learning culture that facilitates professional development and the principles of lifelong learning, and reinforces the need for partnership and multi-agency working. The long-term goals identified by the report are for personalized services designed to meet the needs of those who use them and early intervention rather than crisis management, both of which are to be achieved through integrated services and partnership working. The profile of a competent and confident workforce is again highlighted, linked to performance improvement, and achieved through ongoing education and training and embedding evidence-based practice.

The definition of social work agreed by the International Federation of Social Workers (IFSW) and the International Association of Schools of Social Work (IASSW) in 2001 provided the foundation for these recommendations, outlining the role and purpose of social workers:

> the social work profession promotes social change, problem solving in human relationships and the empowerment and liberation of people to enhance well-being. Utilizing theories of human behaviour and social systems, social work intervenes at the points where people interact with their environments. Principles of human rights and social justice are fundamental to social work.
>
> (Hare, 2004)

The *Changing Lives* report provides a clear statement of social work as a profession, 'underpinned by a common body of knowledge, skills and values, set out in the Framework for Social Work Education in Scotland' (SSSC, 2003) and identified the 'centrality of working for change through therapeutic relationships' (Scottish Executive, 2006: 28) as the basis for strengthening the profession in the twenty-first century. The report described the function of social work being achieved through six core roles: individual case worker, advocate, partner, assessor of risk or need, care manager and agent of social control. Key legislative responsibilities were identified as the sole responsibility of social work – that is, those circumstances where people 'pose a risk to themselves or others or are placed at risk by the actions of others' (Scottish Executive, 2006: 30).

Social work in England and Wales is also preparing for improvements to practice and training, identified by the Social Work Taskforce (SWTF, 2009). The Social Work Reform Board has been created to take forward the 15 recommendations made by the SWTF, many of which mirror those outlined in the twenty-first-century review carried out in Scotland. In addition, however, the SWTF has recommended an 'overhaul' of the content and delivery of social work degree courses, an assessed probationary year post-qualifying and the creation of a National College of Social Work (SWTF, 2009). The SWTF final report, *Building a Safe, Confident Future*, can be accessed at www.publications.dcsf.gov.uk

In both of these review processes the higher education institutions (HEIs) – universities – have been highlighted as having a significant role to play in the delivery of this change agenda. The journey to become a competent and confident professional begins as you enter professional education and training and continues throughout your professional career. This learning environment provides the initial knowledge, skills and values that will become the foundation for future practice, developing a sense of professional identity and professional responsibility. HEIs also have a role, in partnership with service providers, to develop opportunities for practitioners to participate in post-qualifying (PQ) professional development programmes such as specialist training for mental health officers, practice teachers (educators), child protection and leadership training, as well as more general post-qualifying education. Each professional council across the UK will have an identified PQ framework in place that identifies available courses in your own local area.

Professional performance: knowledge, values and professional development

The development of a competent workforce has been the aspiration of governments and the social work profession itself for over two decades. The provision of quality services and a desire to enhance the well-being of those disadvantaged in society are an integral part of social workers' motivation and an influential factor in their self-assessments. It is important to acknowledge the significant difference social workers make in many people's daily lives and, as professionals, we should celebrate these achievements.

Social work can reflect positively on its strengths but also has to continue to develop if it is to secure its place as a credible profession for the future. The demanding nature of social work will not change, and professional responsibilities are unlikely to be reduced, so it is crucial for the profession to actively seek out effective strategies that will enhance their performance beyond functional competence, securing public confidence, creating a positive professional identity and solidifying our confidence to make a useful contribution to society's well-being.

The literature discussed so far in this chapter provides us with some guidance on how to ensure quality professional performance. We have been provided with consistent messages regarding the significant link between acceptable professional performance and key professional features such as:

- the existence of a professional knowledge base that informs practice
- the application of common professional values, and
- a commitment to ongoing professional development.

These key features focus on aspects of professional practice that each of us can take personal responsibility to achieve. For social workers in training these areas form part of the assessment process experienced during practice learning experiences, providing a crucial opportunity for the development of lifelong professional habits as well as evidencing current progress and development in meeting the required standards of practice. Given the significance of these key areas to professional performance, some attention will be given to each, independently, in this concluding section of the chapter.

Professional knowledge

It is not uncommon – for social workers in training in particular – to become confused by the difference between knowledge and theory. For the purpose of understanding the context of professional knowledge we can draw on the work of Walker (1992), Cust (1995) and Macaulay (2000). Initially, however, the *Oxford Dictionary* offers a useful definition of what constitutes knowledge: 'facts and information, and skills acquired through experience or education: the theoretical and practical understanding of a subject' (Pearsall and Hanks, 2003: 967) and a definition of theory: 'a system of ideas intended to explain something' (Pearsall and Hanks, 2003: 1829). Within education and training programmes you will have been introduced to a wide range of scientific, theoretical concepts and research findings, facts and information, which exist to help professionals make sense of situations or events in individual's lives or in society. While these are valuable additions to our knowledge sources, a reliance purely on scientific knowledge to inform practice is limiting as it merely offers a universal explanation that cannot be applied absolutely to each unique individual's experience. When utilizing theory, our task is to be able to analyse and evaluate theoretical concepts in light of its potential application to each unique situation, using it to aid our assessment and understanding, but also taking account of other sources of knowledge. For example, both Fook (2007b) and Trevithick (2008) remind us of the important contribution of 'expert' knowledge that service users and carers can offer to the decision-making process and the wider development of professional knowledge. Fook (2007b) argues that 'scientific knowledge becomes more and more necessary but less sufficient' (cited in Cree, 2011: 32) as we attempt to manage the uncertainty that comes with risk assessment and management.

The *Oxford Dictionary's* definition of 'knowledge' provides a broader perspective that goes beyond acquiring theoretical knowledge. The inclusion of skills development, and the ability to both understand theoretical concepts and directly apply this understanding to inform action, are a significant addition.

The development of professional skills is crucial for effective professional performance and should not be overlooked as they too are informed by theoretical perspectives. Without a theoretical understanding of how to communicate and engage with service users we would be unable to carry out accurate assessments or plan for appropriate intervention. Not only do our skills enable us to carry out our roles and responsibilities effectively, but professional skills –such as reflective practice – enable us to analyse and evaluate theory and research, creating and developing our own 'practice wisdom' (Thompson, 2009; Humphrey, 2011).

Walker's (1992) explanation of 'content' and 'practical' knowledge that informs professional performance offers a perspective that is more relevant to professional practice, but is not dissimilar to that of the *Oxford Dictionary*. Walker's 'content' knowledge includes a range and depth of theoretical knowledge that informs thinking and action, and the 'practical' knowledge refers to the integration and application of this 'content' knowledge, carried out in such a way that is in accordance with professional values (cited in Jones and Joss, 1995: 21). Cree suggests that it is 'better to think of knowledge in general terms which incorporates theory and skill' (2011: 4) and cites the work of Cust (1995) and Macaulay (2000) to highlight the wide-ranging and constantly developing sources of knowledge that inform professional thinking and action.

Cust (1995) suggests that knowledge used to inform action included 'conceptual knowledge' (knowing that), 'procedural knowledge' (knowing how) and 'strategic knowledge' (knowing what to do when) (cited in Cree, 2011: 4). Macaulay (2000) offers additional explanations of these themes by expanding on the sources of each type of knowledge, identifying conceptual knowledge as being informed by 'concepts, facts, propositions and theories' acquired through experience or scholarly activity; procedural knowledge as the 'specific action to be taken when the right conditions are present' and strategic knowledge as 'an awareness of when to use conceptual and procedural knowledge and why' (cited in Cree, 2011: 4).

To ensure that the theoretical concepts that inform our 'content' (Walker, 1992) or 'conceptual' (Cust, 1995) knowledge are valuable and credible, it is imperative that they are underpinned by the best evidence available to us. Evidence-based practice has a crucial contribution to make to the ongoing evaluation of our practice as it offers a basis for decisions regarding 'the appropriateness and currency of our knowledge base' (Sciulli, 2005). Social work practitioners, however, also need to possess research skills in order for them to critically evaluate the wide range of research evidence available to them and require the ability to analyse and reflect on the potential application of research findings with direct practice.

This process of continuously developing our professional knowledge is very much part of the responsibilities that come with professional practice, and is a key factor in professional development. In addition to drawing on research findings, Schön (1983) suggested that professionals themselves were in a position to actively develop their own knowledge base by learning from their practice experiences. This 'learn by doing' (Schön, 1983) approach encouraged professionals to develop their 'art' as a skilled practitioner by applying skills of reflective practice to reconstruct what they know in light of practice experiences and applying the subsequent learning to future practice. Humphrey (2011) offers a similar argument when she talks of the 'practice wisdom' that comes with reflecting on practice experience. 'Becoming a wise practitioner is inseparable from becoming a reflective practitioner' (2011: 92). The 'wise' practitioner is one who has achieved a level of competence and confidence in their professional knowledge, skills and values so they are able to 'adapt their communication repertoires to the needs of service users and carers...dissolve defences which distort communication and understand general approaches to practice and specific intervention techniques so that they can select and apply them correctly' (2011: 91).

For social workers in training the specific initial knowledge required of a newly qualified practitioner is outlined in the QAA Benchmark Statements (2000) which form part of the Requirements (2002) and Framework (2003) for social work education and training. These knowledge requirements are designed to inform the practice outlined in the NOS (TOPPS, 2002) and Scottish SiSWE (SSC, 2003) key roles, and include a wide range of subjects such as law, social policy, sociology, psychology, research, communication and interpersonal skills, methods and models of intervention, interprofessional practice and values and ethics, to name but a few. All of these are regarded as necessary to inform generic, holistic practice and provide a foundation on which to build more specialist knowledge relevant for specific service user groups and services.

The basis of social work expertise lies in our ability to draw on a wide range of knowledge in order to respond to the unique problems our service users face. Our knowledge comes from an eclectic range of sources which are intended to enable us to function effectively in complex and uncertain situations, developing creative solutions that are designed around the needs of the individuals who require our services.

Whether an experienced practitioner or undergoing initial professional training, it is crucial that we all acknowledge and value the significant role that credible professional knowledge plays in providing us with a framework on which to base our thoughts and actions and offers us an ability to justify and articulate our decision to others. 'In the current environment, incapacity to articulate what we know places us at a considerable disadvantage' (Osmond and O'Connor, 2004, cited in Thompson, 2009: 207).

Activity

-   Identify the content, conceptual, procedural or strategic knowledge you currently possess.

Professional values

Professional values are a central feature that underpin all aspects of social work practice, but it would be inappropriate to think of professional values without first considering the role of personal values in professional practice.

Personal values are initially formed during our early socialization process and are influenced both by our own individual experiences and the accepted norms of the society in which we live. Values represent what people consider to be 'good', 'right' or 'normal' and therefore may differ across cultures, and within cultures, due to each individual's experience of gender, age, social class or ethnicity. These beliefs and values are a significant part of who we are as people and influence how we 'tick' and interact with those around us. 'They shape the way we think, the judgements we make and the perceptions we hold about people' (Beckett and Maynard, 2005, cited in Cree, 2011: 130). An individual's personal values may have been one of the drivers that led them to social work as a career choice, and in turn may be influential in determining the kind of professionally qualified social worker they become. However, given the wide range of challenging experiences each social worker will face during their professional career, it is vital that we all take time to acknowledge our own personal values, become consciously aware of what they are and where they come from, so that we can bring this awareness to the reflective process and thereby ensure they do not negatively influence professional practice. It is not possible or desirable to switch off our personal values and there will be many occasions when we will be faced with professional dilemmas due to encountering tension between our personal and professional values, no matter how experienced we become as practitioners. It is for this reason that we develop a level of self-awareness that enables us to think about what is happening to us internally, acknowledging our thoughts and feelings, and developing a new perspective by considering how our personal values may be influencing our perceptions or actions in practice. The professional skill that enables us to do this is reflective practice, but we will consider this in more detail later in the text.

Activity

-   Identify three personal values that are important to you.
-   Who/What has been significant in shaping your personal values to date?

Just as personal values inform our thinking and judgements, professional values provide us with a framework on which to base decisions that are often complex and without clear 'right' answers. 'The ethical documents of a profession thus serve as guidance about the "good" in practice...they also constitute a declaration to the wider society about what can be expected of the "good practitioner"' (Hugman, 2008: 444). The 'ethical documents' Hugman is referring to would include a professional code of ethics and code of practice, both of which inform direct practice and provide clear statements to the public about the standard of service they should expect.

A professional code of ethics consists of 'a set of principles, standards or rules of conduct for ethical practice' (Banks, 2006: 5), their content representing the values of the profession. A code of ethics outlines the 'broad principles' that the profession values and 'highlight potential areas where ethical issues may arise' for practitioners (Banks, 2006: 99).

The IFSW and IASSW (2004) approved a joint statement on ethical principles that were intended to act as a guide for each national social work association around the world, providing a basis for the creation of a geographically sensitive code of ethics, allowing cultural differences to be acknowledged while maintaining shared international beliefs.

The IFSW/IASSW Statement of Principles (2004) identifies two core values:

- Human rights and human dignity – which includes the principles of self-determination, participation and focusing on people's strengths.
- Social justice – which includes the principle of challenging discrimination and recognizing diversity.

The British Association of Social Workers (BASW) Code of Ethics (2002) encompasses these principles in the core values it identifies for the profession:

- Human dignity and worth.
- Social justice.
- Service to humanity.
- Integrity.
- Competence.

Within each country's code of ethics professionals are usually offered guidance on the actions that will promote the application of the core values (Banks, 2006). For example, to fulfil the core value of human dignity and worth, social workers are expected to convey respect for human rights and self-determination; social justice is fulfilled by actively reducing disadvantage and exclusion; integrity is achieved through honest, reliable and confidential services; and to achieve the core value of competence, practitioners are expected to maintain and expand their competence to provide quality services (BASW, 2002).

Having a code of ethics provides a shared set of general principles to aspire to, goes some way to shaping our professional identity and offers us a minimum level of practice that we can measure our practice and our agency's practice against. Banks

(2006) argues that the existence of a code of ethics reminds us that we have a wider responsibility to challenge policy and agency procedures, rather than merely follow them unquestionably.

In addition, the general principles highlighted in the code of ethics provided by BASW and the GSCC Code of Practice for Social Care Workers (2002a) and Employers (2002b), provide social workers and employers across the UK with a list of statements that influence 'the standard of professional conduct and practice required of social care workers as they go about their daily work' (GSCC, 2002a, 2002b). The statements identified for employers require them to adhere to the standards identified in the code, support the workforce to meet the standards, and take action when practitioners are found to have been involved in misconduct or failed to meet the required standard of practice (GSCC, 2002b). The code of practice forms part of the workforce regulation systems, discussed earlier in this chapter. Where practitioners are found not to have maintained expected standards of practice they will be investigated by their professional council and may be removed from the professional register as a result of misconduct, resulting in an inability to be employed in a professional social work role or social care role that requires registration.

Individuals who require social work services have a right to expect a basic standard of service, and the existence of a professional code of practice goes some way to ensuring this occurs by 'drawing a clear line between practitioners' personal and professional lives and requiring them to avoid abusing or misusing their position for personal ends' (Beckett and Maynard, 2005: 80). The code of practice is intended to 'protect and clarify service users' rights and to clarify the roles of the social worker and agency' (Banks, 2006: 99). Each of the statements identified in the code of practice reflects the values of social work and is regarded as promoting the principles identified in the code of ethics. The six statements identified in the Code of Practice for Social Care Workers are provided for you in Appendix 3, but a full copy can be accessed from your local professional council's website. An example of one of the statements for practitioners which is particularly relevant for this text is statement 6: 'As a social worker, you must be accountable for the quality of your work and take responsibility for maintaining and improving your knowledge and skills' (GSCC, 2002a). Fook argues that reflective practice 'makes professional practice more accountable through ongoing scrutiny of the principles upon which it is based' (2007b: 363).

The GSCC Code of Practice actively encourages practitioners to 'examine your own practice and look for areas in which you can improve' (2002a), but each of our ethical documents specifically identifies a social worker's responsibility to actively maintain their standard of practice and competence through ongoing learning and professional development.

Social work duties and responsibilities present practitioners with a range of complex situations where conflict can arise between personal, professional, agency and societal values. Our ethical documents are not intended to provide us with ready-made answers to difficult questions, but by including an awareness of the potential influence of personal values and a knowledge and understanding of the application of professional values in our reflection, alongside relevant knowledge and skills, we can be guided to make informed decisions about the right course of action and be confident in our ability to justify these actions to others.

Activity

- Where might you encounter tension between your personal and professional values?

Professional development

Consistently throughout this chapter reference has been made to the significant role professional development plays in professional performance and competence. This defining feature is arguably the most significant, as without active participation in our ongoing professional development, our knowledge becomes outdated, skills become stale, and the likelihood of unethical practice increases.

Professional development is the activity that enhances the quality of service provision and enables practitioners to manage the complexity, uniqueness and uncertainty that form an integral part of social work's duties and responsibilities. Thompson offers a sobering thought when he reminds us that our level of commitment to continuous development not only influences standards of service, but can also influence the levels of potential 'harm we can do to others' (2009: 207).

It is for these reasons that evidence of our commitment to professional development has become a professional requirement in social work education and training, post-qualifying registration, and is included in our code of practice.

Higher Education Institutions have a responsibility to create opportunities for learners to develop professionally and to achieve this they will generally build a range of learning experiences into the design and structure of their programmes. Social service employers also have a responsibility to facilitate the continuing professional development of their workforce which may involve attendance at internal or external courses or creating learning forums to share 'good' practice. While others have a responsibility to provide you with these opportunities it is each practitioner's responsibility to ensure they engage in a process of learning that will enhance the application of professional knowledge, skills and values and result in professional growth and development.

The initial introduction to professional development may come when you enter professional education and training. This experience may at times resemble a 'magical mystery tour' as, although you are aware of your final destination, you are likely to have times when you feel less confident about your abilities to successfully navigate the obstacles you encounter along the way.

Social work education, in my view, requires learners to undertake two developmental journeys simultaneously, each running in parallel and each influencing the development of the other: one relates to your personal development, challenging you to arrive at a new sense of 'self'; the other is the development of your 'professional self', which will allow you to shape the kind of social worker you will become. Many of the challenges experienced on this journey are influenced by the interaction between your existing personal 'self' and your developing 'professional self' (Wilkie and Raffaelli, 2005: 110).

It may seem a little strange to associate your career choice with personal development, but this is an area that has real significance to your professional performance and overall professional development. Lishman explains the link when she says 'personal development is essential to underpin professional development since our use of self is part of the service we offer to service users and carers' (2009a: 373). To explain this further we can consider the question of why individuals choose social work as a career. What significance does personal motivation have on the kind of professional social worker they will become?

My own experiences of being involved in the admission process for a wide range of social work education programmes have highlighted that prospective social work students are drawn to social work for many reasons. Some individuals are drawn to the social work role because they recognize inequalities in our society and see social work as a means of addressing oppression and discrimination. Some are drawn to the potential job satisfaction that comes from making a positive difference in the lives of those individuals who are marginalized in our society. Others are drawn to the role as a result of personal life experiences, or have in the past been service users themselves. Individual motivation for social work has generated a good deal of interest due to the recognition that this initial driver has an important bearing on each social worker in training's journey to becoming a professional. If you wish to read more widely on the subject, you might be interested in the work of Shaw (1985), Cree (2003), Preston-Shoot (2003) and Humphrey (2011), all of whom present evidence of personal motivation for social work that concurs with my own anecdotal practice evidence.

Personal motivation for social work is relevant for professional development as it can influence how an individual may experience the wide-ranging roles and responsibilities social workers are engaged in. For example, an individual who has a strong sense of social justice would fit comfortably in the role of advocate, working on behalf of service users, but may find it more challenging to function in the role of 'agent of the Court' within Criminal Justice Services, where applying legislation and being an agent of social control are more prevalent.

While many learners bring a strong sense of social justice and valuable life experiences with them to social work education and training, it is equally important to recognize that our motivation to be involved in social work can also include less conscious drivers, which Egan (2007) called the 'shadow side' of helping. Egan defined this as 'all those things that adversely affect the helping relationship' (2007: 25). Some examples of unconscious personal agendas that would adversely affect the working relationship might include situations where there was an unresolved tension between personal and professional values, occasions where judgements were made based on previous personal experiences, or situations where personal solutions to problems are offered to service users. There may also be unconscious personal emotional needs being fulfilled by undertaking a job such as social work – for example, to fulfil a personal need to give of oneself to others, a desire to rescue those in difficulty, or a means of avoiding dealing with one's own problems. Part of the process of becoming a professional social worker will involve exploring and challenging any potential personal agendas, resulting in new levels of self-awareness. Becoming aware of what motivates us, through self-reflection, is emotionally challenging, but an important part of the personal development that is crucial in the journey to become a professional social worker. 'Self-awareness is necessary if we are to recognize our impact on others' (Lishman, 2009a: 375) and how others impact on us.

It is difficult to consider that there may be more to your choice of career than you had previously considered, but we are complex creatures. And though it can be a little unsettling to think that there may be unconscious influences that will impact on your practice in the future, what I would urge you to remember is that the positive motivating factors that brought you to social work are strong building blocks for effective practitioners of the future. Those presently unconscious factors can become conscious through the process of reflection, at which point they can be managed effectively, giving you added insight and enhancing your effectiveness. Lishman concludes: 'We need to develop our self-awareness and capacity for critical reflection in order to ensure that our motivation and past experiences are used to enhance practice' (2009a: 375).

Activity

- Take a moment to record what influenced your decision to choose social work as a career.

- At this time, what might influence your 'shadow side'?

Jones and Joss defined professional development as: 'the method by which professional knowledge and experience are acquired, developed and refined' (1995: 22). Crucial opportunities for professional development come from within a practitioner's own practice experiences. Our ability to 'learn by doing' (Schön, 1983) is not only confined to the development of our knowledge base. Looking critically at what we do also provides us with opportunities to reflect on the application of our skills and values. However, to effectively learn from these experiences, we need to actively take responsibility for engaging in a process that will facilitate 'deep' learning. Jones and Joss (1995: 26) suggested the following process (my comments are offered to help you interpret the concepts):

Analysis	Questioning what to make of something or scrutinizing.
Observing	Seeing peers in role play exercises, colleagues or practice teacher in practice.
Reflecting	Stepping back and considering from another perspective with a view to improvement and change.
Experimenting	Trying out the outcomes of the process so far.
Conceptualizing	Making sense of what you have learned, coming to some conclusions, and embedding these in your future practice.

Activity
– Can you describe an example of this process occurring for you? – Can you identify what aspect of your practice you changed as a result of this learning process? Did subsequent changes result in any improvement of practice? – Which stage of the process do you think was most challenging for you?

In my experience the stage that most social workers in training – and many qualified practitioners – struggle with is that of 'reflection', and therefore their learning and ongoing development will be seriously restricted.

Reflection is, however, the core activity that facilitates professional development. 'We need to develop the discipline of reflecting on what we have done...in order to learn, confirm good practice, analyse mistakes and develop alternative actions and responses.' (Lishman, 2009a: 376).

The process of making sense of our personal and professional experiences and arriving at new understandings is at the heart of this text, but reflective practice can only be an effective process if there is a knowledge and understanding of the concept and a belief that it has a credible place in the development of professional performance and ongoing professional development. The following chapter intends to provide you with an overview of key theoretical frameworks that underpin the concept of reflection in order to develop your knowledge of the subject. Chapter 5 will offer a range of tools to assist your understanding of how this theory may be applied in practice. The content of Chapter 4 has been included to provide you with a knowledge base that will inform your personal development and highlight how the interaction between your personal and professional 'self' influences professional performance.

Summary

This chapter has introduced you to a wide range of topics directly related to key concepts and practice that are relevant for effective professional performance.

You have been provided with a snapshot of the historical events that have been influential in shaping current expectations and standards in professional services, including social work. The evolving social work profession has been briefly presented clearly highlighting the significance of a changing political landscape on the role social work plays in society. Social work is undeniably a political activity, the profession assigned to implement political initiatives, but our uniqueness and greatest challenge come with the moral activity inherent in social work that leads us to search for solutions to those tensions that arise between fulfilling our legal duties and the application of our professional values.

The reform of social work in the twenty-first century has defined the role and purpose of the social work profession, acknowledging the knowledge, skills and values that inform our interactions but identifying the need to work with others to ensure the most vulnerable in our society are supported and protected from harm.

Collaborative and inter-professional practice will require social workers to articulate the knowledge, skills and values that inform their decision-making and be confident of the unique contribution they will make to partnership working.

A clear responsibility has been given to HEIs to provide a standard of initial professional education and training that will ensure that those entering the profession are equipped to competently and confidently carry out their professional roles and responsibilities. The design of professional programmes is intended to reflect the principles of collaborative practice and involve a range of stakeholders, such as service users, carers and social work practitioners in the selection, teaching and assessment of social workers in training.

To achieve a level of professional performance that will ensure secure professional competence and confidence, social work practitioners need to embrace the principles of lifelong learning and actively engage in reflective practice as a means of facilitating their ongoing professional development.

3 Reflection defined

The previous chapter considered the role reflective practice plays in professional performance and identified practitioners' responsibility to embed reflective practice into their working routines.

Each social worker in training is also required to evidence their development as a reflective practitioner as part of their professional training and therefore will be provided with a range of support from academic staff and/or practice teachers (field educators) during their time at university and in their practice learning (field) experiences to assist the development of this professional skill.

It has been my experience, however, that one of the barriers for learners developing this aspect of their practice originates from a lack of confidence in their understanding of the theoretical frameworks that inform the concepts of 'reflection' and 'reflective practice'. For this reason this chapter aims to focus on the work of some of the well-known and respected writers in this subject area. Though it is not possible to provide a full account of all of their extensive works, the chapter summarizes the key theoretical features from some of the early 'masters' – such as John Dewey, Donald Schön and David Boud – who have provided the foundations to our knowledge and understanding of 'reflection', and captures the main themes and perspective presented by those contemporary writers who have contributed new understandings, such as Jan Fook, Gillie Bolton, Jennifer Moon and Neil and Sue Thompson. Providing this overview of the 'old' and 'new' theory that underpins the art of reflective practice hopefully demystifies the process, provides a solid foundation for further detailed reading, and acts as a springboard for your growing confidence as a reflective practitioner.

Many individuals already integrate a degree of reflection in their personal lives, particularly when an event or experience has proved challenging or difficult. Reflection becomes part of their process of trying to understand 'why' events occurred, and for some the outcome of this process will be used to influence future decisions and behaviour. For others, the outcome of their reflection becomes internalized, but not used or valued. Some individuals may prefer to exist in the present and focus on 'doing' – learning and adapting behaviour or actions through trial and error, and spending little time analysing previous events or contemplating their actions. Each of us has our own way of managing our personal experiences, emotionally and practically, and as a result each of us will make different use of personal experiences to shape future events.

Activity
–   What best describes your natural approach? Thinker/Analyser or Active/Do-er? –   Describe one situation when this approach has been useful for you and one where, retrospectively, you think another approach would have been more beneficial. –   What are the advantages and disadvantages of your 'natural' approach?

Schön (1983) was of the opinion that having an experience in itself does not automatically produce learning; this requires a conscious activity that would process the experience and usually result in change. Boud, Keogh and Walker (1985) argued that individuals had different levels of reflective ability, believing this to be a factor that determines those who effectively learn from their experiences. Your preferred personal approach to managing your experiences is relevant to your personal and professional development as this will be influential in shaping your professional journey to become a reflective practitioner. You should not be discouraged if you are not 'naturally' reflective as these skills can be learned. It is important, however, that you are aware of your personal, preferred, approach as the familiarity will seem attractive as you attempt to make sense of your professional experiences. All of us, no matter what our natural preference, are required to develop our reflective skills to a professional level that is appropriate and sufficient to facilitate ongoing learning and professional development.

Before we begin to consider the theoretical basis of 'reflection' and 'reflective practice' it might be useful to initially consider a simple distinction between these two concepts. The process of 'reflection' can be described as the detailed thinking you may undertake about an event or experience, and the new perspective or knowledge you gain as a result of this process. But this on its own will not necessarily improve your professional performance. It is only when the outcome of your reflective thinking is directly applied in practice that 'reflection' becomes 'reflective practice' (Horner, 2004). By committing ourselves to 'reflective practice' we are making a commitment to constantly update our knowledge, skills and application of values through the process of our structured reflection on practice experiences. The reflective process invites change (Mezirow, 1991) and is only effective when new action, or a new perspective, is the outcome. It is this potential for change and development that makes reflective practice so important to your professional performance and ongoing development. The 'reflective practitioner' is one who has fulfilled their commitment to the ongoing development of their practice by implementing change and continually constructing and reconstructing their knowledge and skills in light of their practice experiences.

However, it is important to acknowledge that the process of reflection is challenging, as it heightens awareness of practice conflicts (Mezirow, 1991) and can evoke a range of potentially painful emotions (Rich and Parker, 1995). Creating the time, space and appropriate environment to engage in ongoing reflection will be your responsibility, but you do not have to 'struggle' with it by yourself. During your professional training you will receive help to develop your reflective skills through supervision or tutorials, thereby familiarizing you with developmental and reflective relationships that you may replicate with others when you become a qualified practitioner.

The coach/mentor/supervisor role was important in Schön's (1987)
it helped practitioners to identify and describe practice issues that represe
they did well, and highlighted areas of practice that were in need of deve
The supervisory relationship was particularly useful in helping practitioners
and overcome personal barriers during the reflective process, leading to a heightened
awareness and greater depth of learning to inform future practice. Lishman argued that
'we need to use the experience of training, supervision and our colleagues to help us
examine our ways of dealing with uncertainty and, where they are found to be inappropriate, to explore and practice other ways' (2009a: 380).

Early explanations of reflection

John Dewey (1859–1952) is recognized as one of the early 'masters' due to the important contribution he made to the body of knowledge that informs our understanding
of the concept of learning from experience. His work provided a foundation for the
development of future theories of 'reflection', such as those developed by Schön (1983;
1987) and Boud et al. (1985).

As an educational philosopher, Dewey's interest and research focused on the use of
everyday common experiences as potential sources of learning, including those experiences in which we had had no prior instruction. He was particularly interested in the
connection between what we do, and what happens as a consequence to us or others
as a result of our actions.

Dewey emphasized the importance of adopting a questioning approach when
dealing with challenging situations, developing an attitude of enquiry, and argued
that all learners required characteristics such as 'open mindedness, responsibility and
wholeheartedness' (Dewey, 1933) if they are to effectively learn from their experiences.
For Dewey, the characteristic of 'wholeheartedness' advocated that 'open mindedness
and responsibility' should be central features of a reflective practitioner (Dewey, 1933).
Zeichner and Liston's more recent description of 'open mindedness' was 'the active
desire to listen to more ideas than one, to give attention to alternative possibilities
and to recognize the possibility of error even in beliefs that are dear to us' (1996: 10).
Pollard and Tann (1994) suggested that 'responsibility' involved thinking about the
consequences of practice in personal, academic, social and political areas.

For Dewey, the potential for learning was most likely to arise from experiences we
found challenging. Dewey believed that the means to restore a degree of balance in times of
uncertainty was to be found through the process of reflective thinking. Dewey's early definition of 'reflection' described the process as 'the continual re-evaluation of personal beliefs,
assumptions and ideas in the light of experience and data and the generation of alternative
interpretations of those experiences and data' (cited in Knott and Scragg, 2007: 5).

The 'data' being referred to included information or knowledge that an individual
possessed prior to the experience. By re-evaluating (questioning) what you 'know',
this knowledge or 'data' can be reconsidered in the light of experience, resulting in a
new understanding and perspective. This new perspective then offers the potential to
identify new solutions to the problem situation.

Two further points worth noting from Dewey's definition is the clear message that reflective thinking is an ongoing process, not a one-off occurrence as a result of a single challenging event. The second useful point is that we need to consider how our personal agendas – such as personal beliefs – may influence our interpretation of current events, a requirement featured in our codes of practice (GSCC, 2002a; SSSC, 2005) which will be discussed in more detail in Chapter 4.

To demonstrate the application of Dewey's perspective we might consider an event that occurred early in your course of study, such as completing one of your early academic assignments. This understandably causes anxiety for all learners as they are unsure what is expected of them, and the knowledge they will be required to include in the assignment is usually new and still being digested.

Experience

Submission of academic assignment. Prior to beginning the task you are likely to have considered previous experiences of essay writing, study routines, and may have been given some advice from module tutors in preparation for the submission.

Reflection

Revisit the experience of completing the assignment – what was going on? This process might include revisiting some of the thoughts that were present as you completed the task and some consideration of how these influenced your actions. What messages did you bring with you into university about your own strengths and weaknesses as a result of previous educational and personal experiences? How did the group dynamics, interest in the subject, or attendance impact on your learning and completion of the task? How did your anxiety influence your approach? How did you prepare? Did your study routines work for you? What worked well for you?

Having reflected on your experience, the next stage is concerned with what you do with the new perspective this reflection has provided for you. This next stage in Dewey's approach is known as:

Conceptualization

Consider solutions – how might I use this new information in the future? This is the stage of sorting through the outcome of your reflection and concludes with a range of decisions about how you might do things differently in the future – for example, changes to your time management, where and when you study and write, accessing support from tutors to clarify the task or discuss your understanding of the question or the subject content, accessing library resources and consulting librarians about referencing software, and a decision on when is the best time to do this. Regarding personal agendas, how can you be supported to redress your internal messages? What do you need, how might you get it, who might help you with this, and what might stop you making progress?

Experimentation

Try it out and fine tune. The final stage of this reflective process is for you to prepare to apply the decisions made in the conceptualization stage to a new experience, such as the next academic submission. But first you can experiment by trying out some aspects of your plan or undertaking the preparatory work that might be necessary in advance – for example, visiting the library, participating actively in your teaching modules and accessing tutor support as you require it, negotiating time and space with your family and friends around assignment submission dates and practising your other decisions as and when you can.

Experience

Take the decisions made as a result of completing this process and apply them to the next academic assignment experience to see how they change the experience and, potentially, the outcome.

Dewey believed that the learning achieved as a result of reflecting on our experiences contributed to professional development. This ongoing spiral of learning ensured that professionals, who took time to reflect on their experiences, could continuously reconstruct their knowledge, skills and values in light of the learning they achieved from each new experience.

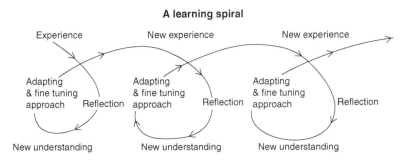

A learning spiral

In a professional context, Dewey believed that we could build professional knowledge and expertise from the experiences presented to us while doing the job (1933). He argued that we achieved a deeper understanding of situations when we had been personally involved in the activity, took time to explore what had occurred, and made use of what we discovered to inform future practice. Without this reflective process, Dewey argued that our practice became habitual and mechanistic (1933).

As a social worker in training you might agree that practice learning experiences enable you to achieve a deeper understanding of the social work role and a growing sense of how your professional knowledge might apply in practice. The danger of mechanistic or habitual practice is, however, a very real dilemma for those who are new to practice as the focus of the work can easily become task orientated or purely functional, rather than engaging with the complexities that come with service users' holistic needs – particularly in situations that are new or challenging. 'Given the anxiety-provoking nature of the situations they face, student practitioners need to embrace reflective learning if they are to avoid becoming restrictive, routinized and ritualistic in their practice' (Ruch, 2000: 108). This dilemma is not, however, confined to social workers in training, as experienced practitioners, who are wrestling with workload pressures and the managerial demands of their organization, face similar challenges.

Beverley and Worsley (2007) suggest that the reflective process itself can offer some assistance in managing the tension between the profession's focus on quality services and organizations' emphasis on procedures and targets. Applying Dewey's attitude of enquiry, individually, or with others, we can reflect on issues such as professional identity, professional values or being part of learning organization. The reflective process can allow us to revisit the consequences of the organizational culture we function within to identify potential consequences and explore possible solutions to resolve professional tensions.

Potential limitations of Dewey's perspective

Dewey's focus on learning from challenging experiences arguably limits our learning opportunities as it excludes those events that result in a satisfactory outcome or pleasure. It is equally important to reflect on positive experiences to ensure we can transfer the knowledge of what we successfully achieved to new situations, as well as identify areas for future development.

Dewey also gave little consideration to the function of professional or technical knowledge in his discussions, focusing more on gathering and accumulating experiences on which to build understanding.

His research was not designed around professional practice and therefore does not acknowledge the complexity and uncertainty encountered when fulfilling professional roles and responsibilities. He did, however, advocate that practitioners should develop an enquiring mind, questioning before accepting, and apply thinking that is based on 'knowledge' and experience.

Dewey's questioning approach placed more emphasis on the cognitive (thinking) process involved in reflection, developing new understandings and interpretations, rather than new action. He acknowledges the potential direction a new perspective can offer, when considering future action, but he did not include an explicit expectation that new action or change would be the outcome of the reflective process.

Activity

– Record your immediate thoughts about what you liked, disliked, already knew and learned having considered Dewey's perspective.

Donald Schön (1930–97), also a philosopher and educationalist, spent time studying and developing Dewey's research findings as he too was interested in how individuals learn from experience. Schön, however, was particularly interested in professionals' ability to 'think on their feet' (1983: 54) in the midst of the ever-changing context of practice. Schön believed that change was a fundamental part of modern life. He proposed that the 'crisis in confidence' experienced by professionals in the 1980s was a result of their failure to find ways to modify their actions to meet the changing needs and expectations of modern society. He acknowledged the 'complexity, uncertainty, instability and value conflicts' (Schön, 1983: 39) that many professionals faced in their daily practice, and argued that managing this reality required a 'system' that would enable ongoing learning and facilitate an ability to adapt practice to suit the changing needs of service users. Schön believed the process of reflection was the 'system' that would enable professions to meet the challenges presented by consistent change.

Schön recognized that professional knowledge was a feature of being part of a profession and acknowledged that technical knowledge offered practitioners the potential to make sense of their work in a theoretical way. Part of the professional 'crisis in confidence', however, was attributed to a lack of confidence in this technical knowledge, which Schön believed was due to a gap between professional 'espoused' theory and the reality of how professionals actually acted in practice. Moon describes 'espoused' theory as 'those theories formally seen by the profession to guide action and encompass the formal philosophy of the profession' (1999: 40).

In Schön's view, technical knowledge was limited in what it could offer professionals as it failed to provide 'ready-made' or 'right' answers to the unique and complex realities of actual practice (1983: 30). Schön (1983) was critical of any suggestion that we could simply apply theory or technical knowledge to practice in a direct way, believing instead that 'we need to integrate theory and practice rather than simply apply one to the other' (cited in Thompson and Thompson, 2008a: 139).

Schön's (1983) interest lay in the quality and the source of knowledge professionals utilized to construct answers that are 'right' for each unique situation they encounter. He was not advocating 'theoryless' practice, or suggesting professionals should not think about what they were doing just because a theory did not neatly 'fit' a situation; he wanted professionals to reflect on what they 'know', drawing on a wider range of knowledge and experience. Schön believed that professionals knew much more than they thought they did, particularly underestimating their practical knowledge, proposing instead that their working life depended on 'tacit knowing-in-action' (1983: 49). The concept of 'knowing-in-action', previously introduced as 'tacit' knowledge by Polanyi (1967), is described as the knowledge we draw on unconsciously and intuitively to inform our actions; carrying out an activity without having to think about it, such as driving or riding a bicycle. Once the initial knowledge has been learned and applied, the spontaneous knowing-in-action enables us to execute the activity competently in the future. The 'knowing' is implicit in the action itself (Schön, 1987: 25).

In a professional context this knowing-in-action develops over time as practitioners encounter aspects of practice repeatedly, resulting in the development of a 'repertoire' (Schön, 1983: 60) of judgements, skills and techniques that they draw on while carrying out their role, without having to think about what they are doing. 'S/he learns what to look for and how to respond; the knowing-in-action becomes more tacit, spontaneous and automatic' (Schön, 1983: 60). As a social worker in training you will have entered your social work course with your own 'repertoire' that has developed from work or life experience, and this will provide the foundation for the new experiences you will have during your social work course, both in university and in practice learning experiences.

While knowing-in-action can lead to the skilful execution of an activity, there are two main areas of concern for this being relied on in professional practice. The first concern is that the unconscious nature of the knowledge embedded in knowing-in-action means that it is difficult for a learner or practitioner to adequately describe what is informing their actions to others; in fact, Schön (1987) highlights that, when asked to do so, practitioners are likely to provide inaccurate information. This inability to describe the knowledge that informs practice may strike a chord for many learners. In my experience as a practice teacher the inability to verbalize what has informed skilfully executed practice has caused anxiety and frustration for many social workers in training during their practice placement experiences. We are, however, accountable for our actions, and therefore our professional credibility is influenced by an ability to articulate and justify our decisions and actions. The second concern relates to the danger that routinized or mechanistic practice will become an acceptable norm, an answer to the challenges of practice demands, thereby ignoring the uniqueness of each service user's circumstances and increasing the likelihood of providing an ineffective service.

The reflective process does, however, reduce the likelihood of routinized practice as it encourages our knowing-in-action to come to the surface and become integrated with our technical and professional knowledge (Schön, 1983).

To demonstrate the application of Schön's explanations let us consider your personal communication skills. You may recognize that you have an ability to engage comfortably in conversation with others, your knowing-in-action guiding what you do. You may have been described as a 'good listener' and 'easy to talk to' but would have struggled to describe to others why this is the case or what you do in conversations that might lead people to describe you this way. The technical knowledge gained through your professional training, however, tells you that the use of 'open' questions and empathic responses will encourage those you are communicating with to share more information and leaves them feeling you understand and are interested in them and their perspective. You will have learned that active listening involves more than the words you hear said, but also includes the use of your observational skills and a knowledge and understanding of your own and others' non-verbal communication, all of which you use to inform what you hear (Lishman, 2009b).

When reflecting on your communication skills the technical knowledge helps you to verbalize and evaluate your knowing-in-action, resulting in the reconstruction of what you 'know'. By integrating your technical knowledge with your knowing-in-action you are bridging the theory–practice gap, enhancing your knowledge and skills to a level necessary to carry out your professional responsibilities. By reflecting on your communication skills you have an opportunity to ensure that your application of these crucial skills are at a level necessary for competent professional practice, which go beyond the skills necessary for daily personal communication. Your competence to engage with service users, carers and colleagues, and your ability to gather relevant information from your interactions, will have a direct impact on the accuracy of your subsequent assessments, which in turn will impact on the quality of your ongoing planning and chosen interventions.

Schön argued that the process of reflection allowed your 'art' as a practitioner to be developed and acknowledged (1983). Reflection both facilitates the building of professional 'artistry' and encourages the integration of this 'artistry' with technical, professional knowledge and ongoing research findings (Schön, 1987). This process of integrating professional knowledge with your knowing-in-action to inform future practice is believed to be the foundation on which professionals develop their own 'informal theory' (Thompson and Thompson, 2008a: 141) which they use to work effectively in situations where uncertainty and value conflicts exist. By reflecting on the application of our knowledge, skills and values in practice we are afforded the opportunity to build and strengthen our own 'professional knowing' (Schön, 1983), also referred to as 'personal theory' (Beverley and Worsley, 2007) or more recently 'practice wisdom' (Thompson, 2009; Humphrey, 2011) .

Schön, however, like Dewey before him, argued that it was more often the 'element of surprise' (1987: 26) that led individuals to reflect – those situations that did not go according to plan or failed to meet our expectations. In these circumstances Schön (1987) believed we could respond to these situations by either choosing to avoid thinking about the experience, or reflecting on the experience in one of two ways: 'reflection-on-action' or 'reflection-in-action'.

Reflection-on-action is described by Schön as the activity of looking back at our actions retrospectively in order to discover how our knowing-in-action may have contributed to the unexpected outcome so that we can prepare ourselves for future actions (1987). Although reflection-on-action can be undertaken individually, this kind of reflection is the form usually used when reflecting with your peers, tutors or practice supervisor. Bolton reminds us, however, that 'self-respect is needed while opening up to close observation and questioning previously taken for granted areas' (2010: 33). Reflection is not intended to make you feel bad about yourself or be seen as a confessional for practice that was less than competent. The opposite is true; reflective practitioners are more confident professionals because they question their actions and have created a sound basis on which to build future practice.

Alternatively, Schön believed that 'thinking on our feet' and our ability to 'learn by doing' suggested that we not only can think about what we have done, but can also 'think about doing whilst doing' (1983: 54). Reflection-in-action enables us to reflect in the midst of our actions: 'action–present' (1987: 26). 'Our thinking serves to shape what we are doing while we are doing it' (Schön, 1987: 26). By questioning the assumptions embedded in our knowing-in-action we can critically evaluate the thinking that led to the situation. The outcome of questioning what we 'know' allows us to reconstruct new understandings which result in a new perspective and the identification of a strategy for new action. Bolton describes the process of reflection-in-action as 'a hawk in the mind constantly circling, watching and advising on practice' (2010: 33).

If we stay with the example of the use of your communication skills you may have found yourself in a situation whereby the non-verbal signals presented by a service user did not correspond with what was being said. In this type of situation your reflection-in-action might initially lead to you to critically evaluate the accuracy of your interpretation of the non-verbal communication. This would include drawing on your professional knowledge as well as your knowing-in-action but, once checked, would lead you to question the underlying cause of this discrepancy. This questioning will lead to a wide range of further evaluation of the situation which requires more information before you could reach any conclusion, but it may also lead you to a new perspective that suggests the service user is experiencing an emotional response to the topic of your discussion. By changing direction and acknowledging their feelings, informed by both your knowing-in-action and your professional knowledge of empathic responses, you are able to both re-engage with the individual and achieve a more effective interaction for both of you. Schön referred to reflection-in-action as a 'reflective conversation' (1987: 31) with ourselves. The significance of reflection-in-action is the potential to have an immediate impact on practice as it is occurring, thereby changing the outcome for the good.

This process can initially sound a bit daunting, especially for those of you who are in the early stages of your professional training, but with your existing life experience and each new practice experience, simulated or real, and the ongoing acquisition of professional knowledge, you will quickly develop a wide range of sources of knowledge to inform your actions and reflections. The important issue is to create a routine of questioning what we know and continually develop our 'artistry' by adapting our knowledge in light of our experiences. La Boskey (1993) argued that 'Alert Novices' were proactive in their reflective thinking as they were constantly questioning practice and were motivated by a will to know 'how' and to know 'how to improve'.

While reflection-on-action cannot offer an opportunity to change practice in real time, it does create an important opportunity to step back temporarily from an experience, to create some space to digest what has occurred, and then to revisit the experience in order to use it to deliberately and consciously inform what we do in the future. It is, of course, possible to use reflection-on-action to reflect further on your reflection-in-action experiences, thereby enhancing your learning and 'artistry'.

Schön's (1983; 1987) perspective offers a message that highlights the importance of developing a balance between thinking and action. Schön (1983) advocates that practitioners need to draw on a range of sources of knowledge, including 'formal' theoretical and research-based knowledge and the 'informal' knowledge gained from practice and life experiences, when attempting to find solutions to the 'messy' complexities of real-life situations (cited in Thompson and Thompson, 2008a). He introduces us to a continuum of reflection that encourages us to integrate our formal and informal knowledge, both during practice and retrospectively, constructing solutions that are client-centred and result in the development of our own personal theories and practice wisdom. A significant factor in Schön's theory of reflection is the action that results from the process. The goal is to challenge ourselves and what we know with a view to ultimately reshaping and reconstructing our knowledge, skills and values in light of our experiences, altering our practice accordingly.

Potential limitations of Schön's perspective

Schön's belief that reflection most likely results from unexpected events, both positive and negative in nature, fails to embed reflective practice in everyday practice routines, despite recognizing the complexity and value conflicts practitioners will face daily. He focuses on the influence of 'knowledge' in the reflective process and gives little attention to the significance of personal or professional values in practice.

Eraut's (1994) criticism of Schön's approach was that it required too much time to execute and, as a result, was unlikely to be implemented by professionals. Time has been identified as a barrier to reflection, but it could also equally be argued that Schön's theory requires less time as reflection-in-action occurs in the midst of practice and therefore requires no additional time, and reflection-on-action can be integrated into ongoing supervision arrangements.

McIntyre (1993) argued that a high level of reflection was only possible from experienced practitioners. This view, however, does not take into consideration Schön's acknowledgement of the important role that mentors/supervisors play in the development of learners' practice and reflective skills. Schön does support the developmental nature of reflective skills over time, at least for those practitioners who practise reflection; otherwise, no matter what your length of practice experience may be, without practice you are not going to develop high levels of reflection.

Hoffman-Kipp, Artiles and Lopez-Torres (2003) believed that Schön had not sufficiently acknowledged the benefits of reflection as a social practice, focusing more on the individual processes of reflection.

Activity

–   Record your immediate thoughts about what you liked, disliked, already knew and learned having considered Schön's perspective.

David Boud, Professor of Adult Education in the Faculty of Arts and Social Science at the University of Technology, Sydney, Australia, has made a significant contribution to our current understanding of reflection.

Boud and Walker (1998), like Schön (1983), believed that having an experience in itself does not necessarily lead to learning, arguing instead that we needed to consciously engage in a process that would help us to extract the learning from our experiences. Reflection, in their view, was the process that enabled an experience to be turned into a source of learning and development. Boud, Keogh and Walker described the process of reflection as 'a generic term for those intellectual and affective activities in which individuals engage to explore their experiences in order to lead to new appreciations' (1985: 19).

One of the longstanding distinguishing features associated with Boud's work was his interest in the role emotions play in facilitating or blocking the reflective process, as outlined in Boud et al. (1985). Miller and Boud proposed that the exclusion of feelings in the reflective process resulted in 'major barriers' to learning and development for professionals (1996: 10). Boud and Walker argued that 'it is common for reflection to be treated as if it were an intellectual exercise – a matter of thinking rigorously. However, reflection is not solely a cognitive process: emotions are central to all learning' (1998: 194).

Boud et al.'s (1985) perspective was built on the premise, similar to that of Dewey and Schön, that the stimulus that led individuals to reflect came from those situations that resulted in some personal discomfort or doubt. Their interest, however, specifically focused on how our emotional responses to these stimuli influenced how we experienced the event itself. In an attempt to help professionals explore this area of their practice, Boud et al. (1985) created a framework for a reflective process that they hoped would encourage emotional awareness and understanding which could then be used to adapt future practice. Their framework highlighted three distinct stages: revisiting the experience to recapture our thoughts, feelings and actions in detail; attending to feelings where we analyse the positive and negative feelings that were present and consider how they may have influenced our interpretation of events and our actions; and finally, a re-evaluation of the experience informed by the outcome of our analysis.

One of the key principles informing Boud et al. (1985), Miller and Boud (1996) and Boud and Walker's (1998) perspective is the view that our learning and development are a personal journey, each of us bringing our own social and cultural context into each new experience. Boud and Walker describe these as 'invisible features' that have a 'profound influence over who we are, what and how we think, and what we regard as legitimate knowledge' (1998: 197). These personal features influence the way we view ourselves and others and therefore will be influential in how we view and act in practice experiences.

Imagine you are working with a family who are experiencing problems with their neighbours due to prejudicial views about their religion/culture/race. Imagine you have personally faced discrimination in your own life and this family's experience reminds you how this felt. You may have experienced a range of emotions such as anger, frustration or fear. In the context of practice these feelings can unconsciously re-emerge, influencing how you respond to the family or how you assess an appropriate way forward. The danger comes from the potential to be directed by your own experiences, projecting your emotions into the family's situation, rather than remaining client-centred. Sparrow suggested that 'in bringing emotions to mind they are refelt' (2009: 568). By reflecting on this experience you have an opportunity to acknowledge your feelings, disentangle them from practice, and consider new approaches.

Another distinguishing feature of Boud et al.'s (1985) framework is the acknowledgement of positive as well as negative feelings in the reflective process. This involves reflecting on the feeling of pleasure or joy that might come with a sense of satisfaction when things have gone well. Ghaye (2011) has written more recently about the positive consequences of re-experiencing past successes and the benefits of refocusing our thoughts away from problems towards new possibilities. By asking positive reflective questions that specifically examine those areas that made you feel good about an interaction, you can identify areas that you would wish to repeat in future practice.

An adaptation of Boud et al.'s (1985) framework will be included for you in more detail in Chapter 5 but, like other reflective tools, it is intended more as an illustration of a process rather than a recipe to be followed and therefore you should not expect the process to always fall neatly into place. Boud et al.'s (1985) framework requires a commitment to ongoing professional development as revisiting our negative feelings is uncomfortable. Gibbs acknowledged this discomfort when he argued that all significant learning 'involved a degree of disorientation and personal threat' (1981: 87). It is also the reason why, initially, this process is likely to be more effective if undertaken with others, such as in supervision, until you become familiar with the process and have learned how to overcome the challenges it presents.

By acknowledging the reality of the emotional responses practitioners may experience while undertaking their social work role and responsibilities, Boud et al.'s (1985) framework offers a useful new dimension to our professional development – one that allows us to integrate the developing intellectual/theoretical understanding with the development of emotional awareness, 'enabling thoughts, feelings and actions to inform each other in an ongoing manner' (Ruch, 2002: 203). We cannot deny the human element that we bring with us into practice; it is this that allows us to empathize with others and drives our sense of social justice, but we do need to develop strategies that enable us to recognize what makes us 'tick' so that we can ensure our needs do not compromise the quality of our practice. 'We may not be in control of responsive feelings and thoughts, but we are surely responsible for our actions' (Bolton, 2010: 5). Chapter 4 will consider the emotional context of practice in more detail.

Potential limitations of Boud et al.'s (1985) perspective

Boud et al.'s (1985) framework of the reflective process clearly focuses on an individual, internal process for each practitioner. This approach may have limitations if it becomes the only approach used for reflection as it does not take account of the wider factors that may be pertinent to collaborative or partnership working. Bolton (2010) encourages us to consider the thoughts, feelings and actions of others, as well as our own.

Boud et al.'s (1985) framework relies on a practitioner being able to give an objective, accurate account of an event, including identifying the emotions experienced, when they 'return to the experience'. This is challenging to achieve, if even possible, as Sparrow (2009) advocates that the memory we return to is likely to be changed as a result of mood or responsiveness to the emotions experienced.

Hardy (2004) questions whether or not individuals are able to reflect until they have achieved the 'higher level skills' required for reflection, such as critical analysis, self-awareness and evaluation. This view may not have taken account of the content of social work education programmes which are designed to facilitate the development of these specific skills throughout your professional training. The development of your reflective skills is also designed to be incremental and runs in parallel to these 'higher level skills' so that you can utilize your newly developed skills as a reflective practitioner when you become a newly qualified social worker.

Boud and Walker (1998) raise concerns about the potential for learners to use reflection frameworks as a checklist to be worked through mechanically, ritualizing the reflective process rather than allowing it to be a process of personal questioning and enquiry. They are particularly concerned about learners who may not be clear about the boundaries of acceptable self-disclosure and confidentiality. These areas will be considered further in Chapter 7 when we consider the roles of supervisor and supervisee, but for now it is enough to say that it is vital that learners are given clear boundaries in these areas at the beginning of the supervisory relationship, are offered a safe environment in which to reflect, and are allowed to come to their own understanding, rather than having others' perspective imposed on them.

Activity
– Record your immediate thoughts about what you liked, disliked, already knew and learned having considered Boud's body of work.

Contemporary explanations of reflection

Having considered the foundation on which our knowledge and understanding of 'reflection' are based, the following section will provide a brief outline of how more contemporary writers – such as Gillie Bolton, Neil and Sue Thompson, Jennifer Moon and Jan Fook – have contributed new understanding to the key themes highlighted by the early 'masters'. These authors have written extensively on the subject of 'reflection', and therefore this summary cannot begin to do justice to their work; but the intention is to allow you to see how early themes have progressed over time.

If we continue Boud et al.'s (1985) theme of including the examination of our personal emotions in the reflective process, then contemporary opinion – such as that of Gillie Bolton – continues to support this view. Bolton agrees with Boud et al.'s (1985) view that strong emotions may block the reflective process, but she offers us a new perspective by suggesting that these 'strong feelings are an indicator of ethical values' (2010: 37). This perspective enables us to make a connection between our personal feelings, which arise from our perceptions about what is important, our personal beliefs (values), and our behaviour.

Having a reflective approach, rather than a mechanistic approach, enables us to manage the ethical dilemmas that arise for us in practice. Reflection allows us to question how our emotions and beliefs affect us, and those around us, so that we can use this new self-awareness to adapt future practice. Bolton (2010) encourages us not to only to reflect on our own thoughts, feelings and actions, but also to use the reflective process to think more widely – to include the thoughts, feelings and actions of those we are working with so that we can learn more about ourselves and the way we relate to others.

The authority and power that come with the social work role mean that, if left unchecked, our practice can become oppressive rather than empowering. Bolton argues that 'reflection is essential for responsible and ethical practice' (2010: 5) as it encourages us to 'challenge assumptions, damaging biases, inequalities and questions behaviour' (2010: 3) that might lead us, unconsciously, to marginalize those with less power. If you wish to extend your reading in this area you will find many additional contemporary writers such as Thompson and Thompson (2008a), Beverley and Worsley (2007), Taylor (2010), Ruch (2002) would also be supportive of this perspective.

Questioning our personal beliefs and acknowledging our feelings is a testing process and, like Boud and Walker (1998), Bolton (2010) acknowledges the importance of learners having confident facilitators to assist them initially with this process. Creating a learning environment that is conducive for reflection is the shared responsibility of both supervisee and supervisor, but this environment should be one that applies the ethical principles that reflection itself is built on, such as, trust, respect, confidentiality and the purposeful expression of feelings (Banks, 2006). The subject of learning environments and supervision will be discussed in more detail in Chapter 7.

If we return to Schön's (1987) concept of a continuum of reflection, during and after an event, Thompson and Thompson (2008a) have developed this theme further by suggesting that we also consider 'reflection-for-action' (2008a: 140) in recognition of the importance of the planning stage of the social work process. Thompson and Thompson argue that reflection prior to an event allows us to 'anticipate problems, avoid mistakes', and facilitates 'better time and workload management' (2008a: 140). In the midst of managing workload pressure or responding to managerial approaches it can be easy to forego this important aspect of practice. Taking time to anticipate what the next interaction in your day might present is time well spent as it allows you to consider what may happen and what you might do (Thompson and Thompson, 2008b). By considering these issues you can reflect on your knowledge and previous experiences to help you prepare for what might come. A word of caution, however, as this is not to suggest that the thinking you undertake in your 'reflection-for-action' should be followed rigidly; you need to be mindful of the dangers of preconceived ideas and remain open to each new situation and prepare to draw on your 'reflection-in-action' (Schön, 1987) to help you respond appropriately to the actual situation you are presented with.

Seidel and Blythe (1996) also offered a contribution to the idea of widening the reflective process by proposing that reflective learners should look:

Backward   Inward   Outward   Forward

Looking 'backward' can be linked to the view of Dewey (1933) and Schön (1983; 1987) retrospectively considering our experiences by reflecting on how our professional knowledge, skills, values and knowing-in-action come together to influence our thoughts, feelings and behaviour, with the purpose of informing our planning for future actions (Thompson and Thompson, 2008a) as well as enabling us to adapt our future practice.

Looking 'inward' can be linked to Boud et al.'s (1985) exploration of personal feelings in the reflective process with the purpose of developing an informed sense of 'self' – one that recognizes and understands how personal emotions and beliefs can affect us and those around us, facilitating ethical practice (Bolton, 2010).

Looking 'outward' can be linked to Boud and Walker's (1998) view that our social and cultural socialization influences how we view others, as well as ourselves, and therefore we need to reflect on our perceptions of others. Bolton (2010) also advocates that we need to consider the potential thoughts, feelings and actions of those around us in our reflection to enable us to develop a wider, outward, perspective.

Looking 'forward' is the goal of reflection. The purpose of all the previous stages is the new perspective and awareness that the reflective process can offer, but this questioning process only has real purpose when it is put to use to transform our thinking and/or action. The forward stage can also include not only thinking about how we might adapt and change, but actually carrying it out, thereby fulfilling our responsibilities as a reflective practitioner.

If you are feeling a little dizzy from the prospect of this multi-directional reflective process, the reality in practice is not as frantic as it may sound. The theory is merely guiding us to the potential for learning and development that the process of reflecting on our experiences can offer us – if we are routinely prepared to ask ourselves reflective questions about what we know, believe, feel and do (behaviour), analyse why this may be the case, consider what the consequences of this may be, and plan for how we might adapt/change our perspective or action in the future. If you wish to read further on the concept of a continuum of reflection, then Bolton (2010), Beverley and Worsley (2007) and Taylor (2006) have also contributed to this theme.

When considering the potential limitations of the early theoretical frameworks that inform our understanding of 'reflection', one of the reoccurring themes has been to question the level of ability or skill required to reflect effectively. This theme has been helpfully considered by Moon (1999; 2004) who introduces us to the idea of 'levels of learning', drawing on the work of Van Manen (1977) who categorized the reflective process into three different modes of reflection. Moon (1999) proposed that the process of 'reflection' did not differ over time or with experience. She believed that the level of reflection achieved by practitioners was developmental, progressing from a process that draws on concrete knowledge to one that could engage critically with complexity and uncertainty. It was not the reflective process itself that changed over time, but the practitioner's skill in applying the reflective process in their practice.

The concept of 'levels' of ability is relevant for all learners who are involved in professional education and training as it is necessary for universities to ensure professional standards are achieved. They do this by identifying assessment criteria for each stage/academic level appropriate to the course being undertaken. By the end of an undergraduate social work education programme, learners are expected to have achieved, and evidenced, a level of competence as reflective practitioners. This is not the same level that would have been expected in Year 1 of their course. Over time, and with the development of knowledge and skills, learners will also develop greater depth to their reflective abilities, but only if they are routinely practising their reflective skills.

Ruch (2002) continues this theme when she argues that a recognized characteristic of reflective practice is the breadth of knowledge that an individual may draw on to inform the reflective process. Over time, this breadth of knowledge expands as a result of reflecting on new learning experiences, thereby encouraging and supporting a greater depth to the level of reflection achieved. Interestingly, Schön (1983) built his theoretical framework around three key types of knowledge which were identified in subsequent literature as: orthodox or technical theory, derived from scientific knowledge (Munro, 1998); practice wisdom or personal theory, derived from the integration of technical theoretical understanding with personal experience over time (Rolfe, 1998); and tacit knowledge (Polanyi, 1967, cited in Ruch, 2002: 203).

This range of potential knowledge is relevant when we consider the three modes of reflection identified by Van Manen (1977): technical, practical and critical reflection, each associated with a different level of reflection depending on its objective and outcome.

Ruch (2000: 101) provides us with a summary of these modes of reflection:

- *Technical reflection* is regarded as a beginning level. It draws on technical knowledge or 'formal' theory to examine skills in order to find solutions to identified problems or challenges.
- *Practical reflection* is believed to be informed by unconscious tacit and conscious technical knowledge and encourages a reflective dialogue between self

and others. By using practical reflection to analyse performance the outcome is intended to be the identification of personal and professional assumptions, personal insight, and the means to modify practice in the future.

- *Critical reflection* is regarded as the highest level of reflection as it seeks to transform practice by challenging existing social, political and cultural conditions which promote some interests at the expense of others. Critical reflection includes the outcomes of the previous two modes, but has the added ethical criteria.

Activity

- Which reflective mode do you believe fits best with your current knowledge and skill?
- What do you need to do to move onto the next level of reflection?

Van Manen (1977) has offered a new continuum of reflection for us to consider – one that provides a sense of development over time, acknowledging the development of knowledge and skills in evaluation, analysis and self-awareness. The critically reflective practitioner signifies the highest level of reflection and is therefore the level that professionals will aspire to achieve over time. As a learner, you can usefully refer to these modes of reflection and types of knowledge on an ongoing basis to self-assess your current levels of reflection and plan your future development as a reflective practitioner.

The 'ethical criteria' included in Ruch's (2000) summary of 'critical reflection' is consistent with the view that values are an integral part of being a professional. Thompson argues that critically reflective practice is 'the basis for anti-discriminatory practice' and 'ethical practice' (2009: 72) as it provides an opportunity for us to question if our values applied in practice are in keeping with our espoused values.

All of the contemporary writers contributing to our current understanding of reflection have identified the 'critical' component as a significant feature in maximizing the effectiveness of the reflective process, despite some differing perspectives. For example, Fook draws a distinction between reflective practice and critically reflective practice (Fook and Askeland, 2006; Fook, 2007b), while Thompson argues that 'all reflective practice should adopt a critical perspective' (2009: 27). Whatever viewpoint you prefer, the additional 'critical' component in reflection offers us a new dimension: one that brings a sociological perspective into the reflective process – the consideration of wider social, political and cultural factors that sustain inequality and disadvantage (Thompson and Thompson, 2008b; Fook, 2010).

The evolution of critical reflection coincides with a time when contemporary practice has struggled to resolve the tension between managerial approaches and the focus on efficiency and outcomes (Gardner, 2009) and professional approaches that are informed by values, creativity, flexibility and person-centred practice (Fook and Askeland, 2007; Thompson, 2009).

Fook (2007b; 2010) believes that critical reflection enables practitioners to engage with the question of 'what matters' in practice and to develop strategies for managing the complexities within organizational cultures. This is achieved by reflecting on our professional values, in particular with a view to questioning 'what underlying assumptions and reasoning are being relied on' (Thompson, 2009: 28) that effectively sustain 'existing patterns of inequality' (Thompson, 2009: 69). The outcome of this critical reflection is considered against our sense of what is important, informed by our professional values, resulting in a new perspective from which we can identify changes to our way of 'doing', thereby improving practice.

A significant feature of critical reflection is the impact of power differentials in interpersonal relationships – a reality for all our relationships with service users and carers. Our aim is to identify and question any deep-seated assumptions we may hold in an attempt to ensure that our practice does not continually reinforce inequalities but enables us to actively empower others. It is the action involved in this change process that leads critical reflection to be regarded as 'transformational', as each new perspective has the potential to lead to change.

It could, however, be argued that all reflection has the potential to be equally transformational if the process applies the key features of cognition (inquiry, questioning, analysis and understanding), an acknowledgement of personal feelings and values, a recognition of their impact on practice, and an active commitment to the application of social work values.

Activity

- Having considered contemporary explanations of reflection, what stands out for you?
- Can you identify recurring themes common to all of the theoretical frameworks discussed?
- Where do you see the main differences between them?

Summary

This chapter has outlined some of the early explanations of 'reflection' and 'reflective practice' and considered how contemporary perspectives have developed earlier key themes over time, shaping our current understanding of the concepts. The process of reflection is a conscious activity that aims to offer a new perspective which can lead to the development of change in our awareness, understanding, or actions. Reflective practice requires practitioners to make use of the outcome of their reflections to improve practice, develop new levels of self-awareness, and deliver ethical practice.

Dewey (1933) advises an attitude of enquiry if we are to achieve new understandings; Schön (1987) encourages the development of professional 'artistry' through a continuum of reflection; Boud et al. (1985) identify learning as a personal journey, highlighting the importance of emotions in the learning process; Bolton (2010) asks us to challenge personal values as a means to manage ethical dilemmas in practice and to widen our learning by considering the perspectives of those around us; Thompson et al. (2008a) expand the concept of a reflective continuum by encouraging us to introduce reflective thinking to our planning, prior to events; Moon (1999) introduced us to 'levels of reflection', providing a sense of progression and depth over time; and Thompson et al. (2008b) and Fook (2010) urge us to use reflection to challenge our underlying assumptions and our application of professional values in practice.

The process of reflection, with its ability to heighten awareness, is challenging in itself, but carrying out new practice or sustaining new perspectives is an even greater challenge. The consistent message conveyed by both early and contemporary writers is that skilful reflection leads to more effective practice and more confident practitioners. Reflection offers an opportunity to re-engage with the 'meaning' of social work and discourages routinized/habitual practice. The early development of your skills as a reflective practitioner will be supported through a positive learning environment and the creation of a range of reflective relationships. Your final goal is to become a critically reflective practitioner but, while on your reflective journey, you still have the potential to use your developing skills to deliver transformational practice.

'Through reflection we can change how we think, feel and behave to better meet the needs of service users and carers' (Knott and Scragg, 2007: 49).

4 Enhancing emotional intelligence through reflection

Fulfilling our social work role requires both cognitive and emotional intelligence as our professional responsibilities are both intellectually and emotionally challenging.

Intellectually we are required to assimilate extensive professional and organizational knowledge, use this knowledge to inform our assessments, planning, intervention and evaluations, and function within complex, constantly changing environments.

Emotional intelligence (EI), however, 'is one of the cornerstones of effective social work practice' (Morrison, 2007: 246). The qualities and skills associated with high levels of EI are particularly valuable for social work practitioners, as individuals who possess such skills are believed to have a greater capacity to relate well to others (Koole, Van Dillen and Sheppes, 2009). This capacity to relate to others is informed by an ability to 'understand both ourselves and others as emotional beings' (Howe, 2008:11) and an awareness of how our emotions affect our thoughts and behaviours (Goleman, 1996).

Our function, and effectiveness, begin with an ability to communicate and engage with others – to develop, maintain and sustain professional and therapeutic relationships that contribute to the care, support and protection of those at risk or in need.

Individuals who require our services are generally facing personal challenges which, in addition to practical difficulties, will result in them experiencing a wide range of emotional responses to their situation: poverty may bring despair or anger, change brings feelings of loss or anxiety (Howe, 2008). The effectiveness of our therapeutic relationships relies on our ability 'to recognize, acknowledge and manage these emotional responses if we are to effectively enable the person to move forward and progress' (Thompson, 2009: 86).

Our involvement in people's lives means we also become active participants (Papell, 1996) in their journey to overcome personal difficulty or effect change in their circumstances. During these interactions it is likely that we will also experience our own emotional responses to the situations we encounter. Our interactions and involvement with the emotional context of practice are what makes social work an emotional activity (Thompson, 2009; Howe, 2008).

Acknowledging and responding to the emotions of others are central features of the social work function, but until recently there has been little recognition of practitioners as 'emotional beings' having their own emotional needs and challenges, or consideration of how their emotions may impact unconsciously on their practice. The emotional context of social work practice is initially experienced by our personal 'self' – connecting with our personal beliefs, values and experiences. These experiences are emotionally challenging but become manageable as we develop personal awareness of our internal mental processes, through our personal development, and develop strategies that maintain our emotional well-being. Learning how to 'care' for ourselves is crucial for effective social work practice. Emotional intelligence enables us to take care of our own well-being and the well-being of others (Freshwater and Stickley, 2004) by encouraging skills that connect our own emotional awareness and management with our ability to respond appropriately to the emotional needs of others. 'If we do not look after ourselves we may become so worn down that we are of little value to other people' (Thompson, 2009: 119).

This chapter aims to highlight the relevance of EI for social work practice and considers the significant role that reflective practice can play in enabling you to become a more effective, emotionally intelligent, practitioner. A brief outline of the knowledge and skills required to competently recognize, acknowledge and manage your own emotions and the emotions of others will be provided, drawing on Salovey and Mayer's (1990) research and Goleman's (1996; 1998) theory of EI, highlighting particularly the key features of 'intrapersonal' and 'interpersonal' competence.

The journey to emotional intelligence

Historically, psychological attempts to understand human intelligence focused on cognitive abilities, such as memory and problem solving (Cherniss, 2000). However, Robert Thorndyke (1921) believed that other factors, such as 'social intelligence', also played a significant part in determining an individual's ability to succeed in life, a view supported by Wechsler (1943) who argued that 'non-intellective' elements, such as affective, personal and social factors, were as relevant as 'intellective' elements when considering intelligent behaviour (Cherniss, 2000). Thorndyke (1921) believed that those who possessed social intelligence had the ability to 'act wisely in human relationships' (Morrison, 2007: 248) by displaying qualities such as sensitivity and empathy (Howe, 2008).

This early challenge to the understanding of human intelligence lost momentum until Howard Gardner resurrected the debate in 1983 when he presented his view that multiple varieties of intelligence existed, one of which he referred to as 'personal intelligence' – a term used to describe those who possessed intrapersonal capabilities, such as how an individual engages with their own emotions, and interpersonal capabilities, such as how they engage with the emotions of others (Cherniss, 2000; Morrison, 2007; Howe, 2008).

Salovey and Mayer (1990), however, were the first to be credited with using the term 'emotional intelligence', which they described as a form of social intelligence 'that involves the ability to monitor one's own and others' feeling and emotions, to discriminate among them, and to use this information to guide one's own thinking and actions' (Morrison, 2007: 250).

Salovey and Mayer's (1990) research, cited in Morrison (2007), suggested that emotionally intelligent individuals possessed both intrapersonal and interpersonal abilities due to possessing skills such as:

Emotional awareness	Identifying feelings in self and others.
Emotional understanding	A recognition of how their own emotional responses may affect their behaviour, and being attuned to the emotions of others.
Emotional management	An ability to adjust, modify and regulate personal emotions and an ability to respond empathically to others.

Salovey and Mayer's (1990) research proved a significant step forward in the arguments for the existence of multiple varieties of intelligence, and their work gave recognition and value to intrapersonal and interpersonal capabilities, creating the central features of EI.

David Goleman (1996) popularized the concept of EI through his book *Emotional Intelligence*. His work contributed to the cognitive/emotional intelligence debate by suggesting that clear thinking and wise decision-making could be achieved by making a distinction between the rational (thinking) mind and the emotional (feeling) mind. Goleman believed that the emotional mind was quicker to respond than the rational mind, 'reacting without taking time for thoughtful analysis' (1996: 291). Historically, the 'thinking' mind was regarded as more valuable as it was seen as the source of logic and rational thought, with the 'emotional' mind being seen as the slightly danger-ous, uncontrollable component that could defy logic or explanation. Goleman (1996), however, believed that both 'minds' could offer useful qualities that would be beneficial to effective interactions with others (Butler, 2007) as long as we ensure that the 'two minds' are 'balanced partners' (Freshwater and Stickley, 2004), one not consistently overriding the other.

In addition to the emotional mind's immediate response feature, such as crying when we are sad, Goleman believed there was a second kind of emotional reaction operating in the emotional mind – one that connects our thoughts with our feelings: 'in this kind of emotional reaction our thoughts play a role in determining what emo-tion will be roused' (1996: 293). Goleman describes this part of the emotional mind as being 'associative' (1996: 294) as it resulted in us re-experiencing the emotions associ-ated with a previously emotionally charged event from our own lives when we find ourselves in present-day situations we perceive to be similar to those of our past. Gole-man (1996) highlighted the potential for these emotional 'associations' to upset the effective balance of the 'two minds' as the 'associated' emotions may result in an indi-vidual reacting to the present as though it were the past without taking time to think about or analyse the event. This emotional reaction is likely to be counterproductive to effective interactions with others as it distorts our interpretation of events and can therefore negatively influence our assessments and actions. We become drawn into 'seeing those things that are in accordance with our own feelings and beliefs' (Hum-phrey, 2011: 170) rather than what is actually happening to others in the present.

Goleman's (1996) view added to the growing literature within psychology that acknowledged the existence of a direct interaction between our thoughts, feelings and actions, one of which, Ellis (1962), will be discussed in more detail later in the chapter.

Goleman (1998) believed that EI was as important as cognitive intelligence, argu-ing it determined the quality and success of our interactions with others; however, he suggested that EI required a range of skills and performance abilities, such as self-awareness, emotional resilience, empathy and conscientiousness (Morrison, 2007). Goleman (1998) strongly believed that developing skills in emotional self-awareness should be a priority as this, in his view, was the key to being able to use emotions effectively to enhance our interactions with others. 'As we develop greater awareness we can begin to regulate our behaviour in order to be more effective, both personally and socially' (Goleman, 1998, cited in Butler, 2007: 42), thereby re-establishing the balance between the rational and emotional minds and avoiding the negative consequences of reacting inappropriately to others due to our emotional 'associations'.

Like Salovey and Mayer (1990) before him, Goleman (1998) argued that emotionally intelligent individuals would possess emotional competence in relation to oneself, which he referred to as 'personal competence', and emotional competence in relation to our interactions with others, referred to as 'social competence' (cited in Butler, 2007). From Goleman's perspective, achieving 'personal competence' required individuals to possess intrapersonal abilities in the specific areas of emotional self-awareness and emotional self-management. 'Social competence' required individuals to display interpersonal abilities in specific areas, such as relationship and communication skills – particularly the ability to respond empathically to others.

If you are interested in exploring the concept of EI further, David Howe's book *The Emotionally Intelligent Social Worker* (2008) offers a full account of the history, underpinning theory, and comprehensive arguments for the relevance of EI to social work practice.

Activity

To explore your current levels of EI, consider a recent conversation/interview with someone who is not well known to you.

- Describe what you were feeling and why you were feeling this way.
- Describe what the other person was feeling and why they may have felt this way.
- How easy or difficult do you find 'tuning into' your own or other people's feelings?
- How easy or difficult do you find managing your own emotions or responding to others' emotions?
- What EI skills would you choose to develop further? Prioritize them if more than one.

The literature describing the concept of EI leaves us in no doubt about the importance of developing our intrapersonal and interpersonal abilities. While these two elements are important in their own right, their connection to one another becomes clearer when we recognize that our capacity to identify, acknowledge and respond appropriately to the emotional needs of others is determined by our capacity to identify, acknowledge and regulate our own emotions (Butler, 2007; Morrison, 2007; Howe, 2008; Thompson, 2008b; Humphrey, 2011).

To fully integrate the qualities of EI we need to understand how the emotional context of practice affects us before we can find a way to appropriately manage the emotions of others (Butler, 2007). While social workers need to be 'clear thinkers', this does not mean that emotions should be undermined: 'social workers need to be able to balance their head and heart' (Thompson, 2009: 214). Social work is an emotional activity (Howe, 2008; Thompson, 2009; Humphrey, 2011), but reflecting on the emotional impact of social work practice on our 'self' is often low down a learner's list of priorities. Once we acknowledge the significant link between our ability to acknowledge and manage our own emotions and our ability to be empathic towards others, EI offers us a new incentive to take care of ourselves emotionally by identifying, acknowledging and managing our emotional response to practice events.

Activity

- What personal benefits and barriers might exist for you if you were to focus on your emotional well-being?

Given that intrapersonal and interpersonal competence are such central features of EI, both of these elements will be considered independently so that you have an opportunity to digest their unique qualities and relevance. We will follow Goleman's (1998) advice and focus initially on the development of intrapersonal competence by considering how we may enhance our levels of emotional self-awareness before giving some thought to the skills that will enable us to self-manage our emotional responses. To begin this process it seems appropriate to recognize some of the most common emotionally challenging situations that practitioners regularly face.

Social work as an emotional activity

Work-related stress is a familiar concept that can potentially result in both positive and negative consequences. Some levels of stress can increase energy, motivation and creativity; you may feel you 'work better' under a degree of pressure. Some practice situations have the potential, however, for less positive outcomes, such as the anxiety or frustration that arises as a result of high workloads, increased levels of bureaucracy, managing the tension between 'ideal' practice and practice reality, complex decision-making or managing risk (Morrison, 2007; Howe, 2008; Henry and Renshaw, 2009; Thompson, 2009). For many practitioners these issues 'go with the territory' and therefore the emotions experienced over time go unacknowledged until they overwhelm or, in more extreme situations, lead to practitioners experiencing stress-related ill health.

We should also recognize that engaging and managing the emotions of service users and carers is emotionally challenging; the continual absorption of others' distress is, in itself, stressful (Howe, 2008).

Service users' circumstances or behaviour can also affect us personally. Service users' vulnerability can generate a strong desire to take action that will protect or rescue them. Alternatively, service users' behaviour may generate a strong desire to punish them for their actions. While rescuing or punishing service users is not in keeping with our professional values, and is therefore inappropriate professional behaviour, a social worker does possess the power and authority to make these actions possible. Practitioners have to find ways to manage these tensions between personal and professional values while still experiencing the original emotions generated by the service user's circumstances or behaviour. The response for some practitioners will be to attempt to deny or suppress their emotions as they believe 'they shouldn't feel this way', rather than recognizing and understanding that they too are emotional beings (Howe, 2008; Thompson, 2009).

It is not unusual for social work practitioners to find themselves working with individuals or families who are experiencing a crisis or traumatic event that they themselves have experienced in their personal life, such as experience of separation, loss or death, abuse or violence, or being the victim of an offence or family breakdown. In the event of this situation arising, it is not uncommon for the practitioner to 'relive' the emotions experienced at the time of their own trauma. Practitioners are expected to possess sufficient skill and awareness to ensure they avoid projecting their own emotional responses onto the service users, but in doing so are likely to undermine their own emotional response, seeing it potentially as a professional hindrance.

One of the most personally challenging experiences for practitioners occurs during situations when tension exists between a practitioner's own emotional needs and the needs of others. Authors, such as Boud and Walker (1998: 197) referred to these unconscious needs as our own personal 'invisible features', and Egan (2007) referred to them as 'our shadow side' – both acknowledging the store of subconscious influences and emotions we have accumulated during our socialization that re-emerge in our relationships with others (Humphrey, 2011). The emotional challenges arising from our own emotional needs will be unique to each of us and can be generated from any practice situation we may encounter depending on our personal 'associations' between present and past experiences (Goleman, 1996).

Thompson helpfully reminds us that our emotional responses 'are not a sign of weakness, rather they are a sign of being human' (2009: 96). It is not in practitioners' interest, or in the interest of those who receive services, to attempt to become 'neutral, disengaged technicians' (Thompson, 2009: 118). To suppress emotions or attempt to disengage from our feelings is more likely to be harmful to ourselves, result in subjective practice, and negatively impact on the quality of our relationships with others. Howe, Henry and Renshaw (2009: 67) argue that by acknowledging our feelings 'we can create a balance between our professional behaviour and personal thoughts and feelings'. Once acknowledged, reflective practice enables us to create 'space and opportunity to examine "uncomfortable" feelings, analyse them and use them to fuel future learning' (Brockbank and McGill, 2007: 252) and practice.

Activity

- What aspects of social work practice have, or might, generate strong emotions in you?
- What feelings did, or might, you experience?
- How have you dealt, or might you deal, with these feelings?

The EI that you already possess may have influenced how you responded to this activity. You may have been able to identify specifically what you were feeling and may have dealt with your feelings by coming to a better understanding as a consequence of analysing why you felt this way. Others may not have been so lucky. They may have identified the feelings but been unsure what to do with them, and others may have been caught in the trap of critical 'self-talk' such as, 'I shouldn't feel this way', resulting in negative feelings about themselves.

The range of emotional challenges encountered in social work practice, and the tension that arises from competing needs, may result in a number of occasions when it is difficult to 'tune into' our feelings. But once we accept that we are 'emotional beings' and give ourselves permission to actively, routinely, ask the question 'What am I feeling?', we can begin to take positive action that supports our emotional well-being and ultimately improves our ability to relate to others.

Having acknowledged the potentially emotionally challenging aspects of social work practice, how then might we ensure we can achieve the levels of skill in emotional self-awareness and self-management necessary for professional practice? In this next section we will consider how reflective practice provides the vehicle to facilitate development in these crucial areas.

Achieving intrapersonal competence: emotional self-awareness and self-management

Personal development is an integral part of our ongoing professional competence as it provides a growing awareness of how our past experiences have shaped our sense of acceptable norms and personal values. Humphrey suggests that reflecting on our own life experiences enables us to extract learning that may enhance our work with service users while simultaneously ensuring we avoid 'projecting our own baggage onto them' (2011: 174).

Emotional awareness is a key part of our personal development. It is achieved by identifying what we are feeling, an understanding of why we are feeling this way, and an acknowledgement of how our feelings are potentially influencing our behaviour. Reflection enables us to 'capture the wisdom of our feelings' and discover aspects of ourselves that help or hinder our interactions with others and usefully guide future practice (Hein, 2006: 4, cited in Howe, 2008: 16).

Taking the initial steps towards discovering aspects of our emotional self is not always an easy task as our 'natural' urge will be to hold onto those familiar 'tried and tested' strategies and beliefs that we have developed to deal with our emotions. These personal strategies will have been strongly influenced by our social and cultural norms which shape our ability to identify or acknowledge our emotional response to events, and determine our willingness to display or express our emotions to others (Thompson, 2009). Our ability to 'control' our emotions is regarded as a positive quality in Western society, and 'being emotional' often carries negative connotations. Many individuals will feel uncomfortable engaging with their emotions as a result of these cultural norms as they may be concerned about their ability to satisfactorily control their feelings, or may fear losing the control they have established over time. Emotions can indeed be powerful, resulting in an intensity of feelings that can take us by surprise, or can be confusing as they appear to be disproportionate to the situation being experienced. At times our feelings may be influenced by thoughts that persuade us we 'should' or 'shouldn't' feel a certain way, or we accept some feelings as inevitable and somehow out of our control.

By denying our own emotional needs, we deny ourselves adequate levels of self-care (Thompson, 2009), but by taking the time to understand our emotional 'self', we give ourselves the best opportunity to find a comfortable and effective approach to managing our emotions appropriately in both a personal and professional context.

Activity
–   What positive and negative influences have shaped your ability to identify, express and manage your emotions?   –   How might these influences impact on your ability to reflect on your emotional response to practice events?

It is not unusual to feel a little apprehensive when beginning the reflective process, but at these times it is important to refocus on the purpose and benefits of this professional activity. The purpose of reflecting on our emotional responses to practice situations is to develop new levels of emotional awareness and understanding and to use this learning to enhance our ability to relate to others (Howe, 2008; Thompson, 2009). The reflective process offers 'an opportunity for "deep learning" (Greenwood, 1998), creating a learning situation that is transformatory, both personally for learners and for their practice' (Freshwater and Stickley, 2004: 95).

The transformational nature of reflective practice has previously been discussed in Chapter 3, describing the change that can occur in our thinking and actions as a result of critically reflecting on our practice experiences. Boud et al. (1985) and Boud and Walker (1998) argued that the reflective process should also encourage the development of emotional awareness and increased levels of emotional insight if it is to successfully lead to new appreciations of practice events. If we are to fully transform our ability to care for ourselves emotionally, and therefore improve our ability to engage with the emotions of others, it is important that we make full use of the reflective process to explore our feelings as well as our thoughts and actions.

Schön's (1983) 'reflection-in-action' provides an opportunity to 'tune in' to our feelings when we are in the midst of practice, affording us an opportunity to question how these feelings might be influencing our practice and encouraging us to alter our actions where necessary to ensure we remain focused on service users' needs. Seidel and Blythe's (1996) view that we should look backwards, inwards, outwards and forward when reflecting, Boud et al.'s (1985) framework for reflection, and Gibbs' Reflective Cycle (1988) all offer a reflective process that allows us to think about our emotional responses in more detail, to critically analyse our emotions and re-evaluate our interpretation of events and our actions retrospectively, affording us an opportunity to achieve deeper levels of emotional awareness and understanding that we can use to transform our future actions.

Acquiring new insight and understanding of our own emotional responses is potentially the most challenging aspect of developing greater levels of emotional awareness. If we are to ultimately find ways to manage and regulate our own emotional responses, we need to probe a little deeper and explore our own unique 'invisible features' (Boud and Walker, 1998: 197) to understand those personal influences that create our sense of 'self'.

Our sense of 'self' has been strongly influenced by our unique personal experiences and interactions with others (Howe, 2008). From our formative years to the present day, our contact with others has reinforced or challenged the personal beliefs we have about ourselves, others and our world. By achieving greater emotional understanding we have an opportunity to consider how these personal beliefs may be influencing our present feelings, thoughts and actions, to question their origins and make informed decisions about our future actions. Using critical reflection to explore our early influences we can achieve a deeper understanding of these personal beliefs and ensure our personal issues do not lead us to unconsciously do harm to service users (Thompson, 2009) and avoid 'misusing our position for personal ends' (Beckett and Maynard, 2005: 80). The questioning, analytical nature of reflection is designed specifically for this purpose, providing a framework that enables us to explore and express what we are feeling and why, and to continually challenge those things that are 'dear' to us (Zeichner and Liston, 1996) with a view to reshaping our personal perspectives in light of new experiences (Schön, 1983).

One of the benefits of professional education and training is that we are consistently being introduced to a wide range of technical knowledge that can inform our interactions and interventions with others. This professional knowledge makes a crucial contribution to the quality of the reflective process generally, but it is important to remember that it can also be utilized to enhance the depth of your personal reflections. Cognitive learning theory, which informed psychology's understanding of human behaviour, resonates with Goleman's (1996) theory of the 'associative' nature of the emotional mind which leads us to re-experience past emotions in the present. This subject can usefully inform the development of your emotional understanding by offering a theoretical base from which to analyse and evaluate your emotional responses, thereby enhancing the outcomes of your reflections and highlighting areas you may wish to target as part of your emotional self-management in the future.

Cognitive learning: guiding emotional self-awareness and understanding

You may of course be familiar with aspects of behavioural psychology if you have already considered behavioural approaches as methods of social work intervention, or more generally from your psychology teaching during your social work education and training programme. Behavioural approaches are usually applied to situations where behaviour change is the goal as these approaches work from the basis that behaviour is learned, and therefore can be unlearned, creating an opportunity to adopt new behaviour in the future.

Generally, behavioural psychology has afforded us the opportunity to understand human behaviour using four classifications or types of learning. Early explanations pointed to 'classical', also known as 'respondent', conditioning, which identified an automatic response to certain stimuli – for example, fear results in physiological changes in the body such as increased heart rate and body temperature. 'Operant', also known as 'instrumental', conditioning, proposed that desired behaviour could be strengthened through reinforcement – for example, providing rewards for desired behaviour increases the likelihood the behaviour will be repeated (MacDonald, 2007). Bandura (1965) added cognitive factors to our previous understandings and introduced us to the potential of 'observational learning' – for example, learning by observing others and repeating behaviour observed highlighted the potential for behaviour to be learned without automatic stimuli present and without the need for reinforcement. Our early understanding of cognition (knowing) was informed by Albert Ellis's (1962) interest in how an individual's internal, cognitive processes may influence behaviour. Cognition, as described by Grant, includes 'activities such as thinking, perceiving, evaluating and judging' (2010: 1). Cognitive theory, however, did not achieve full recognition within psychology, or social work, until the late 1970s, which coincided with the development of a range of intervention approaches designed to manage and change behaviour; known as cognitive behavioural approaches. These approaches to change were directly informed by Ellis's (1962) early beliefs that personal mental processes played a key role in the experience of emotions – particularly distress, anxiety and guilt.

Ellis's (1962) theory advocated that our cognitive learning produced 'core beliefs' which were formed early in life and continually shaped and reinforced throughout our childhood experiences, 'underpinning the way we view ourselves, others and our world' (Clifford, 2010: 59). These 'core beliefs' essentially created our own personal rules about how we, the world and life ought to be, and resulted in 'programmed' patterns of thinking which were often negative or self-critical. Despite 'core beliefs' being created from childhood perceptions, and therefore being potentially inaccurate or biased, these negative and self-critical ways of thinking are believed to be 'well established' by adulthood (Clifford, 2010: 60). Ellis's theory argued that the emotions experienced during an event were directly linked to these personal 'programmed' patterns of thinking.

Event -------- Core beliefs --------- Thoughts -------- Feelings -------- Actions

Any event in the present may activate these established patterns of thinking; but what is significant is that the event itself is arguably not what determines how an individual feels. It is our evaluation of the event, how we personally interpret the situation, based on our 'core beliefs', which triggers what we think about during the event. This then influences how we feel, which then determines how we subsequently behave or act.

Ellis's (1962) theory provided new insights into human behaviour, one which acknowledged that behaviour is often influenced by how we feel. By identifying and understanding the origins of these emotional responses, Ellis (1962) believed that action could be taken to modify behaviour by challenging previously established 'core beliefs' and self-critical patterns of thinking.

Activity

Think about a situation where your perception of what occurred differed from others who were also present (e.g. a friend passes you in the city centre without acknowledging you, or a service user is verbally aggressive towards you during a joint visit).

- How were you feeling in the situation you describe?
- Describe why you were feeling this way. What were your thoughts?
- How did you behave the next time you were in the company of this person?

If you consider the scenario of a friend failing to acknowledge you in a social situation it may have resulted in you thinking you had been purposely ignored, and left you feeling uncomfortable or upset by this possibility, wondering what you had done wrong to merit this behaviour. Generally the upset may arise from your uncertainty about being liked by the friend or regarded as important to them. These thought processes may lead you to respond in a number of ways when you next meet, possibly ignoring your friend, or challenging them for not acknowledging you. Alternatively, you may have responded totally differently to this event by thinking they had been distracted by something else and had fun with it when you next met. According to Ellis (1962), your experience of this event will be determined by your 'core beliefs' influencing how you interpret the situation. For example, in the initial scenario the feelings experienced would be influenced by a need to be liked and a sense of how awful it would be if you were no longer friends with this person or found yourself with no friends. The alternative scenario is an example of a situation where your interpretation of the event did not trigger any irrational 'core beliefs'.

This simple scenario may result in friction between friends, but if we consider Ellis's (1962) theory in the context of the power and authority afforded to social workers and consider the complex and challenging responsibilities that are integral to the social work role, the potential consequences of allowing our 'invisible features' (Boud and Walker, 1998: 197) to go unchallenged are much more serious for our service users. The social work role empowers us to have a significant impact on the lives of those in receipt of our services, and therefore if a practitioner is someone who becomes frustrated by events, or upset by service users' behaviour that they believe to be unacceptable, they are in a position to choose how to 'fix' the situation by finding solutions they regard as appropriate. By responding to these personal thoughts and feelings, the practitioner disempowers the service user and is less able to complete accurate assessments that focus on the service user's needs, thereby reducing the likelihood of appropriate intervention being identified. Reflective practice usefully encourages us to question our personal perceptions and responses to events, allowing us to explore personal emotions and achieve clarity in our thinking and future actions.

Ellis (1962) argued that events that caused anxiety or distress were more likely to trigger irrational core beliefs. While humans develop both rational and irrational 'core beliefs' during their childhood experiences, it is the irrational beliefs that lead to self-defeating thoughts and feelings. Our rational beliefs are regarded as being more fluid, signified by our wishes or preferences, but also include healthy negative emotions such as sadness. In contrast, however, our irrational beliefs are regarded as rigid as they come from patterns of thinking that are driven by a sense of 'must', 'should' or 'ought to', which rarely leaves room for the influence of external factors to be considered – for example, 'I should be able to make a difference in people's lives' or 'There's no room for error in my practice.'

After many years of applying their theory in practice, Ellis and Harper (1975) identified what they believed to be the ten most common human irrational beliefs. These are not intended to be seen as concrete, absolute statements as individuals may experience a 'core belief' to different degrees:

Always   ------------   Regularly   ------------   On occasions

depending on how previous personal experiences in adulthood have resulted in successful challenges to old thinking patterns or led to the reinforcement of early core beliefs.

Ellis and Harper's (1975) ten most common irrational beliefs:

1   The idea that it is necessary for an adult to have love or approval from those they regard as significant.
2   The idea that one should be competent and achieving in all possible respects.
3   The idea that when people act obnoxiously and unfairly you should blame and damn them and see them as bad or wicked individuals. Also known as 'damning'.
4   The idea that it is terrible, horrible or catastrophic when things are not going the way one would like them to go. Also known as 'awfulizing'.
5   The idea that human happiness is externally created and that people have little or no ability to control or change their feelings.
6   The idea that if something is, or may be, dangerous or fearsome, one should become preoccupied with it or upset about it. Also known as 'catastrophizing'.
7   The idea that it is easier to avoid facing life's difficulties and self-responsibilities than to undertake more rewarding forms of self-discipline or new challenges.
8   The idea that the past is all important and that because something once affected one's life, it should do so indefinitely.
9   The idea that people and things should be different from the way they are and that it is terrible if solutions to the realities of life are not immediately found.
10 The idea that happiness can be achieved through inaction or passively enjoying oneself without committing to others.

Activity
–   Pick three of Ellis and Harper's (1975) common irrational beliefs and consider how they may influence a practitioner's practice.

In completing this exercise you may have considered how the need to be liked may influence our ability to say no to service users, or make us feel a need to do things for them, rather than enabling them to do things for themselves. This can result in creating dependency on services. Alternatively, if we were driven by 'perfection', then we are less likely to be able to accurately judge our own or service users' successes, which in turn results in inaccurate assessments and a lack of clear decisions regarding an appropriate way forward.

Having considered Ellis and Harper's (1975) ten most common irrational core beliefs, it might be useful to consider examples of some of the most common self-defeating thinking patterns that may present themselves as a result of these internal messages, as outlined by Clifford (2010). Potential links to Ellis and Harper's (1975) common core beliefs have been added to the summary of Clifford's (2010) work in an attempt to help you make a connection between core beliefs and thinking patterns.

Common self-defeating thinking patterns (Clifford, 2010: 63)

All or nothing thinking: with this pattern comes an unwillingness to accept the existence of a middle ground. Instead, things are measured as success or failure, right or wrong. Individuals tend to give up on things rather than accept any error or imperfections. You might think of situations where you decided to eat healthily or stop smoking, but gave up attempting the change in behaviour after the first relapse in your new routine, criticizing yourself for your lack of apparent success and feeling negative about yourself. Potential core belief source 2:4:7.

Mental filler: with this pattern comes an unwillingness to accept the positive, preferring to focus on negative aspects of an event. Information received will be undermined or disregarded if it does not fit with the established personal core beliefs about 'self' – particularly relevant to an individual's sense of self-confidence and self-worth. Imagine your practice teacher praising your skills at the end of a first practice placement and acknowledging your lack of practice experience at the beginning of the placement. This pattern would lead an individual to ignore the positive feedback about their achievements and focus on the identification of their lack of experience, resulting in negative feelings about themselves, the placement, and potentially the practice teacher. Potential core belief source 2 and 9.

Minimization: with this pattern an individual would minimize the importance of things, particularly their feelings. Imagine two friends agreeing to meet for a meal, but one did not turn up or call to cancel. The response to friends is likely to be 'It doesn't matter', despite feeling let down and possibly angry. This pattern is fuelled by self-defeating thoughts that they are not important enough or a good enough friend. Potential core belief source 1:3:4.

Labelling: this pattern of thinking leads individuals to engage in disparaging self-talk which undermines their self-esteem and self-worth. They are usually overly critical of their own performance and have a tendency to undermine their abilities. Imagine failing an assessed task on your course; this thinking pattern is likely to result in derogatory internal messages such as 'I can't do this' or 'I'm not good enough' and can result in a loss of self-confidence, leading to poor decisions about a useful way forward. Potential core belief source 2:4:6:7.

Personalizing: with this pattern individuals will usually accept responsibility for any situation that did not go according to plan, or was perceived to be unsuccessful, despite there being other factors that may have been equally influential. These individuals tend to accept blame, even for situations they are not responsible for. Thoughts of 'It's my fault' or 'It must be me' signify their initial response to events that cause discomfort. Imagine a service user indicating they no longer wish to continue voluntary contact with you due to support being offered by another service. This thinking pattern would lead to thoughts that see the reason for this change being linked to some failure in your actions or personal abilities, rather than a situation that may have been encouraged by another worker in the best interest of the service user. Potential core belief source 1:2:4.

Should statements: these thought patterns describe the unconscious demands individuals place on themselves, but are also examples of critical inflexible thinking which is not only applied to oneself but to others. Typical phrases such as 'Ought to', 'Must', 'Must not', 'Should', 'Should not' or 'Have to' are influential in how situations are perceived. When situations are not experienced as they 'Should be', according to the rules adopted as a result of our core beliefs, then feelings of anger and frustration follow, either directed inwards to themselves or externally onto others. Imagine going into supervision with your practice teacher/assessor with thoughts of 'I must not make a mistake', or coming out of supervision thinking your practice teacher 'Should have been more supportive'. Potential core belief source 1:2:3:4:6:8:9.

These self-defeating thoughts only act to undermine our self-esteem, self-worth and self-confidence as they generate negative feelings about 'self' and others. These established 'core beliefs' and thought patterns 'determine how we judge ourselves and relate to others' (Clifford, 2010: 59) and therefore have the potential to make a significant impact on the quality of our practice.

As you read through the summary of Ellis and Harper's (1975) common core beliefs and Clifford's (2010) common thinking patterns, it is possible you were checking to see which of these you recognized as familiar internal messages of your own.

Activity

- Make a note of the core beliefs that you recognized as personally familiar.
- Make a note of the thinking patterns you recognized as personally familiar.
- Make a note of the personal feelings you think may accompany these thought patterns.
- When you feel this way, how might you behave or act?

Beck (1995), cited in Constable (2007), believed that our core beliefs were so deep-rooted that it can be difficult to acknowledge them to ourselves or others. Reflecting on our thought patterns, and identifying the critical 'self-talk' that accompanies these thoughts, uncovers the beliefs we hold about ourselves (Constable, 2007) and can therefore be extremely challenging. It is important that you don't become disheartened or concerned if you personally recognized a number of the core beliefs or thought patterns as this is very much part of being human. This process can become part of a constructive, positive, step forward in the development of your emotional awareness and heightened understanding of your emotional responses to practice events. It is also important to accept that we all have our own vulnerabilities, and it is unlikely that we will ever successfully eradicate our personal influences. We have already acknowledged that social work is an emotional activity and, as a result, social work practitioners will experience a wide range of emotional responses to practice events. How we manage these emotions, relate to others, and evaluate our own practice are crucial factors that determine our effectiveness. But mistakes and inefficiencies do happen; perfection is not the goal, as it is unachievable. As learners and professional social workers we recognize that our work demands high standards, but the fear of making a mistake can result in routinized practice. This may feel 'safer', but is unlikely to be in the best interest of service users or likely to encourage the development of professional confidence.

We can learn to accept our emotional responses to practice situations and can learn to recognize the link between our feelings and our own personal 'programmed' beliefs and thoughts. It is the personal nature of our emotional response that requires each of us to have the courage to explore and challenge our interpretations of events so that we can begin to make a distinction between our 'ideal', 'should/ought/must be', and realistic practice. Recognizing our own limitations and human frailties is also an important part of becoming a competent professional. Equally important is our commitment to a reflective process that enables us to identify, acknowledge and manage the emotional responses that arise as a result of our cognitive learning. Through reflection we can take care of our own well-being and minimize the potential impact of personal agendas on professional practice: 'to think about yourself and your rules for life, to gain a richer sense of who you are and what motivates you' (Taylor, 2010: 39) to be a professional social worker.

While reflective frameworks – such as Boud et al. (1985) and Gibbs (1988) outlined in Chapter 5 – provide a useful structure for the reflective process, the outcome of your reflections will be greatly enhanced when you use professional knowledge, such as cognitive learning, to inform the analysis of your feelings. The new perspective you will achieve will allow you to monitor and, where necessary, regulate your practice appropriately. Accepting support from others, and functioning within a learning environment that is conducive to transformational learning, will play an important part in the development of your emotional understanding.

Activity
– Having considered the processes of emotional awareness and emotional understanding, identify your key areas of learning.
– Identify your areas for further development.
– What do you need to do to facilitate this development?

Achieving greater awareness and a new understanding of our emotional responses to practice situations can be an empowering experience as it creates an opportunity to take control of previously unconscious mental processes and allows us to transform our thinking and behaviour in the future. It is likely that you already possess self-management skills, but it is important that you can enhance your existing abilities in order to ensure you can effectively manage the new challenges that will arise due to your enhanced emotional self-awareness and practice experiences. Taking responsibility and control of our future actions is very much at the heart of EI's second component of intrapersonal competence: self-management.

Emotional self-management

Having achieved adequate skills in emotional awareness and emotional understanding, self-management is fundamentally the process of taking control of our feelings, impulses and behaviour during our interactions with others (Howe, 2008; Koole et al., 2009).

Emotional self-management encourages us to be aware of all of our emotions – both positive and negative – and to use this awareness to choose how we react and express our feelings. There are times when it is acceptable to allow emotions to control our behaviour, such as in times of joy, pleasure or happiness, but it becomes less acceptable if our behaviour is controlled by negative emotions such as anger, frustration or fear. When we emotionally self-manage, we regulate how, when and where we express our feelings (Howe et al., 2009) so that we can ensure we 'display an appropriate emotional response that is proportionate to the situation we are facing' (Howe et al., 2009: 69). Our emotional awareness and emotional understanding provide the focus for areas that require 'managing'. This is then achieved by adjusting, modifying and regulating our reactions and emotional responses (Cherniss, 2000; Howe et al., 2009) rather than being distracted by our own feelings or reacting impulsively in practice situations.

Activity

- What causes an impulsive emotional reaction in you? What makes you 'lose it'?
- How do you generally respond to others when you feel this way?
- How would you like to modify your response when you feel this way in the future?

If we are to successfully regulate our emotional responses, then we need to develop our ability to build in time between our feelings and actions so that we can reflect on the event and decide on an appropriate response (Humphrey, 2011). Having used reflective practice to become aware of and understand our emotions we now utilize reflective practice to enable us to consider new actions – to help us make decisions about how to modify, or adjust, our reactions, responses and behaviour by asking reflective questions such as 'How might I modify my practice?', 'What adjustments do I need to make to my current practice?', 'How should I regulate my behaviour in the future?', and then to put these new appreciations into practice.

A defining feature of reflective practice is to effect change in our behaviour and actions before, during, or after an event. Being 'tuned in' to our emotions allows us to recognize in advance how we feel about many practice situations, and therefore by reflecting on these emotions we are able to take more responsibility to prepare and plan our actions, ensuring our responses are not driven by impulse or unconscious personal needs. By continually monitoring our emotions we can also ensure that we can actively check our behaviour during an interaction, paying particularly attention to the emotions we may be conveying through our non-verbal communication. Reflective practice, undertaken after an event, allows us a deeper evaluation of actual events, highlighting new areas of emotional awareness that may require further analysis to achieve new understandings before identifying ways to regulate practice in the future.

Howe argues that 'many of the most difficult and intense emotions are experienced when relationships are not going well' (2008: 181). These situations often result in learners feeling at their most vulnerable and therefore more susceptible to old irrational core beliefs being triggered. When the outcome of reflection highlights the emergence of old self-defeating thinking patterns or negative self-talk, the regulatory process can benefit from an 'ability to soothe ourselves' (Butler, 2007: 42) by developing newly constructed positive self-talk that provides counter-arguments to contradict old negative patterns of thinking. These counter-arguments can be developed over time and should draw on previous adult experiences that offer concrete examples and evidence that challenge the accuracy of previously held irrational beliefs, enabling us to modify our negative automatic thoughts (Beck, 1976). Once we become open to the process of self-awareness and emotional understanding we have the capacity to re-educate our 'rational mind' through this process of cognitive restructuring, replacing old thought patterns with new, changing how events make us feel, and adopting new behaviours as a result.

Activity

- Consider Ellis and Harper's common irrational core beliefs or Clifford's self-defeating thought patterns that seem familiar to you and identify examples where your beliefs or thoughts have proved to be inaccurate.
- How does this new perspective make you feel about yourself?
- How might this influence your behaviour in the future?

In my experience of working with learners, the most common cause of distress and anxiety centred on the completion of assessed tasks. This anxiety often triggered critical core beliefs about their ability to successfully achieve an acceptable standard of work, and self-defeating thoughts, such as mental fillers, would undermine the positive feedback offered, choosing instead to focus a disproportionate amount of attention on the areas highlighted for development. Using reflective questions learners were able to acknowledge their feelings, understand the sources of these feelings, recognize how they were influencing their behaviour, and identify evidence to counter old core beliefs and thoughts from previously 'successful' achievements which subsequently improved their confidence in their own abilities.

Critical self-talk affects our mood, which in turn can affect our ability to self-manage our emotions effectively. While this self-talk has a negative impact on how we feel about ourselves, it can also negatively influence our ability to gather information, inhibit clear thinking, influence decision-making (Morrison, 2007; Howe et al., 2009) and have a negative effect on other people. To avoid these negative consequences it is crucial that we create the time and space needed to identify and understand our personal 'invisible features' (Boud and Walker, 1998: 197) so that we can actively take control of these previously unconscious emotional responses by replacing negative self-talk with positive messages that allow our sense of self to grow and develop in confidence and competence.

Service users are 'highly attuned to the emotional demeanour of those they depend on' (Morrison, 2007: 253) or those who have power and authority over aspects of their lives. It may seem obvious to say that it is not appropriate to convey anger, fear, anxiety or distress during our interactions with others; but it is equally important to remind ourselves how effectively these and many other emotions are conveyed non-verbally, through our posture, facial expressions, or tone of voice, as well as directly though what we say or do. By finding ways to 'tune in' to our own emotions and regulate our practice accordingly, we can then focus more specifically on others, engaging in 'purposeful conversations' (Davies, 1985, cited in Coulshed and Orme, 2006) that make service users and carers feel valued, listened to and understood.

Achieving self-management is challenging as it requires us to change behaviour that comes 'naturally' to us, and therefore it is only likely to be successfully achieved when we are open to change and committed to regularly monitoring our practice. The responsibility for maintaining the necessary commitment that will ensure this becomes an integral part of the ongoing process of personal development lies with each individual learner and practitioner. The motivation to practise and persevere with the process of change will be determined by whether you believe the goal is achievable and how much you value what can be achieved.

Activity

- What might motivate you to develop your self-management skills?
- What factors might reduce your motivation?
- What would help you to overcome these demotivating factors?

Taking responsibility for the development of your intrapersonal competence does require time and effort, but this investment allows you to reap the rewards associated with both attending to your own emotional well-being and enhancing your ability to relate to others. Before moving on to consider the second element of EI, interpersonal competence, here are some brief focal points to help you achieve emotional self-management:

- Routinely 'tune in' to how you are feeling.
- Make time to reflect on your emotions and develop strategies to adapt and modify what you do and how you react.
- Take experiences you perceive as critical and reconstruct them to draw out constructive comments that may be helpful to you.
- Create new thoughts – when you identify emotions and reactions that are unhelpful in a practice context, then work to replace them with new positive actions.
- Practise, practise, practise putting new actions into practice.

Achieving interpersonal competence: identifying and responding empathically to the emotions of others

Our own journey to becoming more emotionally self-aware provides us with valuable insight that increases our ability to recognize and understand the emotional responses of others. By regulating our own emotional responses we become more able to 'tune into' the emotions of others and increase our capacity to appropriately manage the emotional exchanges that arise during our professional interactions.

The ability to identify, acknowledge and respond appropriately to the emotions of others is the final key feature of EI and inextricably linked with social work's function to facilitate change through therapeutic relationships (Scottish Executive, 2006a).

Our ability to develop therapeutic relationships is crucial to good quality service delivery and positive outcomes for those receiving services (Morrison, 2007). To be successful, these relationships require us to apply a range of communication skills that support interpersonal interactions, particularly the skill of empathy and an ability to respond empathically to others' emotions. Empathy is described by Howe (2008: 173) as the ability to 'see and feel the world from the other's point of view'. To achieve an understanding of a service user's world, Egan suggests we need to practise 'empathic listening' (2007: 80), which requires us to tune into the expressed emotions, observe non-verbal emotional cues, and listen to the key thoughts, ideas and perceptions being communicated to us. Understanding a service user's experience in this way enables us to complete more accurate assessments and identify appropriate intervention strategies. But we need to do more than listen and understand; we need to convey our understanding by responding to the underlying 'messages' (Egan, 2007: 102) being expressed. Responding empathically is the skill that allows us to 'appropriately manage' the emotions expressed by others through the communication of our understanding and acceptance of their emotional experience. Egan (2007) outlined a 'beginner's basic formula' which allows learners to convey the essence of the understanding they achieved from empathic listening. Egan's (2007: 102) formula consists of two basic statements:

You feel......... (name the emotion expressed by the service user)
because......... (indicate the experience, thoughts or behaviour that gave rise to the feeling).

When we initially translate our perceptions and understanding into words it is important that we present our thoughts in such a way that we have an opportunity to check their accuracy; otherwise we run the risk of leaving service users feeling misunderstood. By presenting the empathic response as a question, service users have the opportunity to think about their feelings and correct any potential inaccuracies in our understanding; but, in doing so, they can also achieve clarity in their own thoughts and feelings – for example: 'it sounds as though you were feeling......... because.........?'

When developing our empathic skills it is important to be mindful of the difference between sympathy and empathy. Sympathy refers to sharing feeling with others (Thompson, 2009) – being sad, angry or frustrated together. While practice events may bring many occasions when we experience a similar emotional response to those experienced by service users, our emotions, if left unregulated, will cloud our thinking and behaviour and result in us being less effective in our role and less able to remain focused on the service user's needs. Our aim, therefore, is to be empathic, which allows us to be sensitive to service users' emotions without taking their feelings onboard ourselves (Thompson, 2009).

It is not unusual for learners to feel apprehensive about engaging with service users' emotions due to concerns about their ability to manage and respond appropriately. Not to engage with the emotional context of service users' lives, however, means we run the risk of appearing insensitive to their needs and increases the likelihood that we will overlook crucial factors that will have a bearing on a successful outcome being achieved. Reflective practice offers a major contribution to the development of professional confidence as it allows us to critically evaluate our practice on an ongoing basis, encouraging us to draw on professional knowledge to assist the development of our communication skills, and ensuring we recognize our ongoing progress.

Service users consistently tell us how they valued the relationship they had with social workers who displayed high levels of communication skills, such as active listening and empathic responses (Spratt and Callan, 2004, cited in Morrison, 2007). Service users appreciate having time to think about themselves 'to attend to feelings, particularly when their feelings are not judged but simply accepted' (Howe, 2008: 183). Our interpersonal skills form the basis of 'effective help' and 'successful' outcomes from a service users' perspective as they evaluate their contact with practitioners on an emotional level (Howe, 2008) – 'How does contact with this professional make me feel?'. Our empathic skills enable us to identify, acknowledge and understand the emotions of others, and allow us to respond in a way that is 'deeply comforting' (Howe, 2008: 173) to service users, creating a strong foundation on which to build and maintain effective therapeutic relationships.

For social workers to successfully enable and empower individuals to effect change in their lives, they require the necessary skills to build and maintain therapeutic relationships. These therapeutic relationships enable us to encourage service users to explore their situation and achieve new understandings that allow them to make decisions for the future. To achieve this goal we need to create relationships that are built on trust, genuineness, acceptance and an understanding of the emotional context of each individual's experience. 'To be genuine implies a willingness to express feelings, acceptance relies on managing competing emotions and empathy is the key skill for handling emotional matters' (Brockbank and McGill, 2007: 54).

The emotionally intelligent social worker recognizes how emotions affect thoughts and behaviours and, as a result, actively seeks to identify, understand and regulate their own emotional responses in an attempt to minimize the potential impact of personal influences on their professional practice. The knowledge and insight achieved as a result of this process enhance a practitioner's capacity to 'tune in' to the emotions of others, to understand their significance and draw on their empathic skills to ensure an appropriate response. By developing their intrapersonal and interpersonal capabilities, learners can ensure they develop their EI to a level that positively influences their professional competence.

Activity

- Which aspects of emotional intelligence stand out for you?
- Which intrapersonal and interpersonal skills do you already possess?
- Identify areas for further development.
- What do you need to do to facilitate this development?

Summary

Emotional intelligence is as important as 'regular' intelligence as it determines our ability to relate well to others (Koole et al., 2009). Social work practice relies on our ability to relate to others, so embedding the qualities and skills of EI in our practice offers an important opportunity to enhance the quality of our interactions and encourages us to create a space in which we can usefully take 'care' of ourselves.

Achieving adequate levels of self-awareness and managing personal emotions and the emotions of others is a major challenge for all social workers and requires ongoing motivation, open-mindedness and acceptance of our own vulnerabilities and limitations. Reflective practice provides the vehicle that facilitates the ongoing development of our emotional intelligence by creating 'emotional thinking' (Howe, 2008) time that aims to enhance our intrapersonal and interpersonal capacity. Investing time in the reflective process enables us to develop new awareness and understanding of our emotional responses, helps us to monitor and regulate our thoughts and behaviour, and provides a springboard to transform our future practice.

5 Reflection applied

Having identified the relevance of reflection for high-quality professional practice and considered the role reflection plays in facilitating personal and professional development, this chapter aims to focus on factors that may hinder and help your attempts to ensure reflection becomes an integral part of your practice routines. Reflection is a conscious activity that allows you to extract learning from your experiences; but you can only achieve this if you are able to effectively carry out the task of reflection. The chapter will highlight the more common obstacles that can deter practitioners from engaging in reflective practice and consider potential practical solutions that will enable you to avoid these common difficulties impacting on your own reflective practice. For those in the early stages of their development as a reflective practitioner it can be difficult initially to determine 'how' to begin the reflective process. So this chapter will also provide you with a selection of structured, practical, activities (frameworks) designed to facilitate the reflective process, allowing you to experience the potential application of the knowledge outlined in Chapter 3, and create a solid foundation on which to build your developing confidence and competence as a reflective practitioner.

Beverley and Worsley (2007) argued that to fully integrate reflection in our professional practice we require a shared professional sense of 'reflection'. For learners who are developing their reflective skills, and having to provide evidence of such to others, reflective frameworks offer a useful resource that may allow the profession, and individual learners, to begin to achieve this goal. It is, however, important to recognize that these structured tools are not intended to become recipes to follow in the long term, but instead should be regarded as a means of developing reflective techniques and confidence that will encourage skilled reflection and reflective practice to become embedded, routinely, in your professional practice over time.

An extensive range of reflective tools currently exists. These are easily accessible by exploring *models of reflection* using reputable internet search engines. Whichever reflective tool you choose to apply it is important to remember that ultimately you are aiming to learn from the experience you are reflecting on, and therefore to maximize this learning you need to ensure you choose a tool that is up to this job. Ultimately you are aiming to ensure that your reflections 'adopt a critical perspective' (Thompson, 2009: 27).

Many reflective tools share a general design, created around some basic common themes, that focus on the cognitive (the content), conative (the action or the process) and affective (the feelings) reflection of an event (Brockbank and McGill, 1998). The most useful reflective frameworks will capture the important features of the reflective process by creating a structure that will encourage users to 'Select an event; Describe, Analyse and Interpret the experience; Explore alternatives and Decide on new actions' (Jasper, 2003: 12). The purpose of a reflective framework is to prompt your thinking, analysis and evaluation of an event through a series of structured, open, reflective questions that will lead to 'a deeper understanding of the experience' (Beverley and Worsley, 2007: 115), which in turn is then utilized to effect change in future thoughts, feelings and actions.

In its simplest form the selection of an event encourages learners to make a considered choice about which experience they wish to reflect on so that they have a clear purpose and focus for the reflective process. Questions such as: 'What do I hope to achieve from this reflective process?', 'What areas of my practice do I need to develop?' and 'What experiences might facilitate this development?' can act as a guide to identifying a suitable source that meets your own needs. Once an event has been chosen, describing the event enables you to take a step back from the experience to consider 'What happened?', 'How did I carry out my task?', and 'How was I feeling?'. Replaying the details and recapturing the experience retrospectively, without judgement, often highlight aspects of the experience that had previously gone unnoticed. The analysis undertaken is a time to question your perceptions of the experience, to consider 'why' you thought, felt or behaved the way you did and question the potential influence of wider issues pertinent to the event, such as personal agendas and organizational, cultural or ethical factors. The outcome of this part of the process becomes the material that is used to interpret the experience by considering '*What* do I know?', '*What* do I aspire to?' and developing a new perspective by comparing your previous actions with your 'ideal' actions. Achieving this new understanding of the experience allows you to consider alternative courses of action for the future, identifying both strengths and areas for development by questioning 'What might I do differently?', 'What aspects of practice should I retain?', 'How might I address.........?', before making a final decision about which actions will be embedded in future practice and deciding 'how' you will carry this out. The process of reflective practice is complete when the learning achieved from this experience is carried through to future practice.

The process described is, however, more appropriate for reflections undertaken after an event – reflection-on-action (Schön, 1987) – but it is still possible to engage in a process of cognitive, conative and affective reflections prior to an event – reflection-for-action (Thompson and Thompson, 2008a) – or even during an event – reflection-in-action (Schön, 1987) – with some minor alterations to the reflective questions being asked. For example, prior to an event you may ask yourself reflective questions as a means of preparing for the event and avoiding potential problems such as:

What do I hope to achieve?
What do I need to do to achieve this?
What do I know that might help me achieve this?
How will I know if I'm not achieving this?
What am I feeling? How might these feelings influence my practice?
What should I do if.........?

During an event you can ask yourself some simple questions that are guided by your observational and listening skills and can facilitate useful 'reflective conversations' (Schön, 1987: 31) that can offer the potential to alter practice in the midst of an event, such as:

What am I seeing? What might this be telling me?

What am I hearing? How does this fit with my observations?

What am I noticing?

What do I know that can guide how I respond to what I am seeing, hearing or noticing?

How am I feeling? How am I presenting? How am I engaging with the service user's feelings?

It is not uncommon for learners to be concerned about their ability to formulate appropriate reflective questions, but this skill will be easily achieved with time and practice. What is more significant is for you to remain focused on the purpose of the reflective process and remember to engage with all of the key components that contribute to professional practice, such as professional (technical) knowledge (Munro, 1998), personal theory (Rolfe, 1998), or practice wisdom (Humphrey, 2011), professional skills, an acknowledgement of personal feelings, and recognition of their impact on practice, and an active commitment to the application of professional values. By questioning, analysing and understanding how these components come together to create your own unique practice, you begin to open the door to learning about yourself and how you function as a social worker. To help you begin to access all of the components that contribute to your practice, Brockbank and McGill (1998) suggest asking open questions that are framed around the 'six wisemen' – What, When, Where, Who, How and Why – to prompt the reflective process and encourage you to look beyond the procedural nature of your practice. You will see these prompts have been used repeatedly in the suggested questions presented for you in this chapter and you will come across them in many of the reflective frameworks currently in use.

Overcoming obstacles

The full benefits of reflective practice will be experienced in time if you embed reflection into your working routines (Taylor, 2010). For those who are developing their reflective knowledge and skills, or struggling to maintain reflective habits, the true value may still be elusive. During professional training you are required to commit time and effort to reflective practice, but as the assessment and monitoring associated with the role of learner comes to an end, the personal decision and responsibility to actively commit to the reflective process fall entirely on you. You will be faced with new challenges and competing demands as a newly qualified social worker, and this period of time may present an early obstacle that challenges your personal commitment and motivation to the process of reflection. During this new experience you will make your earliest professional decisions and will be looking for strategies that help you deal with the new environment you find yourself in.

While reflection offers you an effective strategy to manage this change you will have to decide for yourself how much you value the contribution reflection has to offer; and you will have to decide if you believe this time is 'worth the effort'. This can become an unhelpful cycle as the value of reflective practice will only be experienced once an effort has been made to grasp a sound knowledge and understanding of the reflective process and this understanding has been competently applied in practice.

As a learner, it is difficult to grasp the long-term significance of investing time and energy in the development of reflective practice during your professional training as it can be lost in the midst of the very many other outcomes you are attempting to address. Be in no doubt though that if you choose to invest the time necessary to achieve a sound grasp of the reflective process while involved in education and training, then you will very quickly recognize its value, acknowledge it is worth the effort, and be better prepared to overcome future obstacles that you may encounter once embroiled in professional practice.

Activity

- What currently motivates you to undertake reflection?
- What currently demotivates you about the reflective process?
- What might change your motivation levels?

Three of the most common, self-reported, obstacles preventing practitioners from engaging in reflective practice are: insufficient time, lack of confidence and non-reflective working environments. Having been alerted to these potential challenges provides an opportunity to give some prior thought to how best to avoid or overcome these obstacles if encountered in your own practice.

Social work practitioners face numerous practical and emotional demands and, as a result, have to prioritize and carefully plan their activities in order to meet the needs of service users and the requirements of their organization. It is not surprising then that practitioners might argue that they do not have time to reflect on their practice as they are busy 'doing the job' (Thompson and Thompson, 2008b; Taylor, 2010). It is possible, however, that, in the midst of these work demands, giving yourself time to step back and think may allow you to recognize that by focusing on 'doing' you are not investing time to take care of yourself, personally or professionally, and to consider the potential consequences of these actions. By giving yourself time to reflect, you increase your efficiency, as it helps you to remain focused, and increase your effectiveness, as it ensures your actions are informed – both crucial elements when time is limited. Given the demands on your time it is vitally important that you carefully plan 'how' best to integrate reflective routines efficiently into your practice. Thompson and Thompson (2008b) offer the practical suggestion of building in reflective time before and after an event, adjusting your diary and workload management systems to facilitate this time. Creating reflective opportunities that fit within your working routines can also ensure reflection finds a place in your practice – for example, creating time for reflective discussions in team meetings or as an ongoing part of professional supervision.

The second common obstacle experienced by practitioners is associated with a lack of confidence in one's ability to competently undertake the reflective process. This lack of confidence can be the result of misunderstanding the reflective process itself (Thompson and Thompson, 2008b), anxiety about possessing an adequate level of professional knowledge and skill to carry out the task (Thompson and Thompson, 2008a), or being apprehensive about exploring personal experiences or sharing concerns with others (Thompson and Thompson, 2008b; Taylor, 2010). Taylor acknowledges the problem and provides an answer when she says that it takes 'courage to look at yourself and your practice' (2010: 43) and suggests it becomes less frightening when you recognize 'sequential courage' (2010: 44) will suffice – just mustering enough courage necessary to enable you to take a step-by-step approach to moving forward and effecting change.

It is highly likely that most practitioners will experience a 'crisis in confidence' on a number of occasions during their professional career, but the question remains: Why do some practitioners muster the courage to reflect on their practice and others do not? It does take courage to be prepared to recognize your own limitations, and it takes strength to admit errors of judgement or moments of uncertainty, uncomfortable experiences that will be familiar to every social worker. All of us have to learn how to reflect, just as we have to learn all of the other necessary professional knowledge and skills needed to undertake our role and responsibilities. Allow yourself the time needed to develop the knowledge and skills that enable you to function as a professional. The motivation to overcome this obstacle comes from a positive attitude to ongoing learning and development, recognizing the clarity, direction and control reflection offers, and an awareness of the professional stagnation that may occur if opportunities to question what informs your own practice are rejected.

Having identified a plan of how best to integrate reflective routines in your practice and developed a good foundation knowledge and understanding of the reflective process, one final obstacle that may present itself will come from the working practices and culture of the organization you are working within. Some organizations will actively encourage reflective practice, while others will focus their attention on fulfilling responsibilities for targets and outcomes at the expense of approaches that support critical reflection of 'how' goals were achieved. It is equally possible that you could find yourself in a team where there is little evidence of reflective practice, or even overt undermining of its value.

To find the courage and determination to fulfil your commitment to reflective practice in such working environments is difficult, but not impossible. Thompson and Thompson helpfully remind us that 'the culture may seek to influence our behaviour but [does] not determine our behaviour' (2008a: 144). Engaging in reflective practice is each individual social worker's professional responsibility, and so it is important that you actively develop strategies that enable you to fulfil these professional responsibilities as well as the organization's requirements. Where the working environment is not supportive of reflection, Thompson and Thompson (2008a) suggest seeking out

like-minded individuals from within the organization, or creating supportive alle-
giances with others to manufacture your own learning community. Where possible, it
can be helpful to promote the benefits of reflective practice within your team or organization – for example, by identifying potential common themes that will attract both the
organization's and practitioners' interest. One such requirement is that practitioners are
accountable to their organization and their professional body for the quality of their
practice. One of the many benefits of reflective practice is that it allows practitioners to
substantiate how the decisions they have made and the actions they have taken have
been informed by professional knowledge and supported by a credible evidence base.
By discussing your reflective journey, the positive consequences of reflective practice
and modelling good practice in organizational events, such as training days or supervision, professional colleagues acquire information that may offer them a new perspective which creates potential opportunities for change within teams and organizations.

Reflective tools

Having a range of appropriate reflective tools can also help you overcome the obstacles
you may face as they offer an opportunity to become more confident in your knowledge and understanding of the reflective process and facilitate the development of
reflective skills.

The tools provided for you in this chapter should be regarded as an introduction
to structured reflective activities and will include examples of both early and contemporary design. These tools have been specifically chosen purely on the basis of the
positive feedback they have generated from learners that I have worked with directly
in the role of tutor, mentor or practice teacher (field educator). Hopefully you will find
them equally useful.

The tools provided for you are:

Borton's Framework Guiding Reflective Activities (1970)
Adaptation of Boud, Keogh and Walker's (1985) Reflective Process
Gibbs' Reflective Cycle (1988)
Holm and Stephenson's (1994) Reflective Activity
Critical Incident Analysis Framework (Crisp, Green Lister and Dutton, 2005)

Borton's Framework (1970)

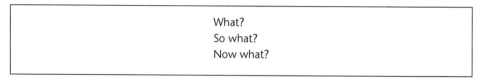

What?
So what?
Now what?

The apparent simplicity of this framework is potentially its attraction as it is easily
remembered, accessible and achievable. But, as with all reflective frameworks, their
simplicity can be deceptive as they serve a very clear purpose – to move away from

purely descriptive or practical thoughts and actions so that we can learn from our experiences through the process of reflection.

Borton's (1970) framework guides us to describe an experience (What?), analyse the experience (So what?) and identify an action plan as a result of the learning from this experience (Now what?). To do this successfully, however, you need to formulate appropriate reflective questions that will allow you to explore the experience in such a way that it leads to a deeper understanding of the events and offers a new perspective that informs your future thoughts, feelings and actions.

Activity

–   Identify two reflective questions that would prompt your thinking for each of Borton's stages.

You may have considered questions such as:

What was my goal? What did I do? What was I feeling? What was good or bad about the experience?

So *what* is important about this experience? So *what* knowledge can inform my understanding of this situation? So *what* have I learned about myself?

Now *what* can I do to improve my knowledge/skills? Now *what* do I need to do to modify my practice? Now *what* do I need to do to achieve this?

Borton's (1970) framework is designed for reflection-on-action, but with practice, and some minor alterations to the reflective questions asked, it can also be usefully applied to facilitate reflection-for-action (Thompson, 2008a) and reflection-in-action (Schön, 1987).

Adaptation of Boud, Keogh and Walker's (1985) Reflective Process

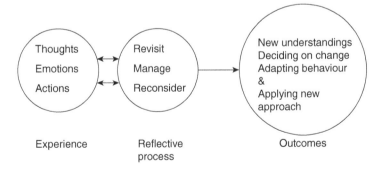

Boud et al. (1985) believed that to effectively learn from our experiences, the reflective process should consider our emotional responses to events, paying particularly attention to how our emotions influence our interpretation of events. Their approach to reflection supports the principles of cognitive theory by acknowledging a connection between our thoughts, feelings and actions. Recognizing that we are emotional beings, Boud et al. (1985) looked for an approach that would facilitate the development of emotional awareness and encourage professionals to find a way of working with their emotions, rather than suppressing or denying the emotional context of their work.

Boud et al.'s (1985) reflective process was designed to facilitate learning from an experience that had resulted in some discomfort and is intended to be undertaken after the event. The aim is to focus on the feelings experienced during the event and to use the analysis of these emotional responses to effect change in levels of emotional awareness, achieving a new perspective and identifying potential future actions.

This adaptation of Boud et al.'s (1985) reflective process is constructed around three interconnected stages: revisiting an experience; managing the feelings aroused during the experience; and reconsidering the experience in light of the new information gathered from the previous two stages. The outcome of this final stage will be determined by the level of recall achieved in Stage 1 and the depth of analysis completed in Stage 2. The overall outcome of this reflective process may lead to change that is not immediately obvious to others as the areas changed by the process may be found in attitudes, values, emotional state or confidence levels, all areas that will indirectly improve practice.

Let's consider each of the stages in a little more detail.

Revisiting the experience

The task in this stage is to recapture the experience in as much detail as possible, paying particular attention to what you were thinking, feeling and doing before and during the event. It is important to avoid making judgements, if possible, and to focus your attentions on 'tuning in' to the positive and negative emotions experienced. Prompts might include: What happened? What was I thinking when.........? How did I feel when.........? What did I do well/not so well?

Managing the feelings

Having identified the positive and negative emotions experienced around the event, the task in this stage is to draw on your knowledge to help you to analyse these emotions so that you heighten your emotional awareness, increase your understanding, and develop greater insight of their influence on practice. Prompts might include: What knowledge can help me understand these emotions? How did my thoughts make me feel? Why was I feeling.........? When I was feeling......... what did I do?

Drawing out the positive emotions is equally important for your learning as it allows you to recognize the things you did well and appreciate the feelings that accompany this behaviour. These positive feelings will increase the likelihood of repeating the action and lead to an increase in your professional confidence. You may wish to reread the section on cognitive learning in Chapter 4 to assist you with your analysis of the negative emotions experienced by considering the potential influence of personal core beliefs and self-defeating thought patterns.

Reconsider the experience

The task in this stage is to re-evaluate the experience in light of the new information and awareness gained from the previous stages. Prompts might include: How does this new awareness change my interpretation of the event? How did my feelings influence my practice? How might I modify my practice in future? What was the service user's experience? What did I learn about myself? What wider issues might be relevant to this situation? What should I do next?

In recognition of how challenging reflecting on the emotional context of practice events can be, here is a brief illustration to assist your understanding of the process.

You are reflecting on an interview with a service user who has repeatedly failed to keep previous appointments with you. You feel positive about finally having an opportunity to talk to him and happy that you have been able to reinforce the importance of maintaining contact with you. You are feeling angry that he is not taking his responsibilities seriously and frustrated by the time you have wasted by his previous non-attendance. In addition to identifying your feelings the reflective process has highlighted that the tone of the interview was punitive, conveyed by your non-verbal and verbal communication, giving a clear indication of your dissatisfaction. His actions have resulted in you thinking that he is 'not motivated', which resulted in you considering withdrawing further support.

Having time to revisit the event allows you to recognize how your feelings of anger/frustration have potentially driven the experience, influencing your behaviour and thinking, rather than enabling you to objectively consider what factors may be influencing the service user's behaviour. A fuller analysis of the event can be achieved by drawing on your knowledge of cognitive theory to provide a more in-depth understanding of the interaction of your thoughts, feelings and behaviour. This knowledge source may highlight that your interpretation of the event was influenced by a core belief such as 'awfulizing', which led you to think it is better to give up, rather than accept imperfections or 'personalizing' the experience by deciding a personal failure on your part has resulted in the non-attendance.

Alternatively, you may be influenced by 'should statements' that determine how the behaviour of others is interpreted: 'He must attend – otherwise I can't be successful.' In this analysis, the thoughts around the non-attendance for appointments has led to negative feelings about self or the service user – in this case, feelings of anger/frustration. The wider issue that requires some further consideration in this situation is one of 'power', which a social worker has the capacity to misuse by withdrawing services or communicating inappropriately, and is therefore in conflict with professional values. This new perspective offers a significant opportunity to reconsider your actions the next time you feel angry with a service user.

As you can see, it can be an uncomfortable process, but the opportunity to make positive changes to your thinking, feelings or actions is very important. Muster the courage – it will be worth it.

Gibbs' Reflective Cycle (1988)

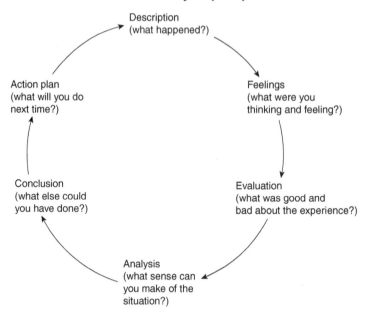

Reproduced with kind permission from the Oxford Centre for Staff Learning and Development

Gibbs' Reflective Cycle (1988) provides a structure that guides you through the reflective process by identifying six key stages that, when explored sequentially, can come together to provide insights that have the potential to contribute to the development of new perspectives and plans for future action. Presenting the process as a cycle reminds us that the reflective process is continuous, signifying that each experience has the potential for new learning through further reflection.

It is important to explore each stage independently, and Gibbs has offered an initial question to prompt your thinking each step of the way. Like Boud et al. (1985), Gibbs specifically encourages you to consider your personal feelings and thoughts, but in this instance they form only one part of the reflective process. With some minor alterations to the reflective questions being asked at each stage, this framework can also be usefully applied prior to and during an event, as well as retrospectively.

Let's take a moment to look a little closer at each of the elements in Gibbs' Reflective Cycle and consider how they come together to facilitate the reflective process.

Description of the experience

At this stage your task is simply to take yourself back to the experience you wish to reflect on and create an account that describes the details of what happened. You should try not to make any judgements or draw any conclusions about these details at this early stage.

Just revisit the experience, using prompts to help you recapture what was going on. You could ask questions such as: What was my role? What did I plan to achieve? What did I do? Who was present? What was their role? What did they do? How did it end?

Feelings

At this stage your task is to recall what you were personally feeling and thinking before, during and after the experience. Once again, try not to make judgements or attempt to analyse; just recapture the feelings and thoughts openly and honestly for yourself. Prompts might include: What was I thinking about this situation before I arrived, during the event, after the event? What was I feeling before, during, after the event? What do I think about those who were present? How did others make me feel? How did the ending make me feel?

Evaluation

At this stage your task is to make value judgements about the experience, using prompts to help you consider: What was good and bad about the experience? What did I do well and not so well? What did others do well or not so well? What turned out as expected or was not as expected?

Analysis

At this stage your task is to make sense of the experience by drawing on your professional knowledge, practice wisdom, self-awareness and professional values to analyse the personal and professional picture you have recreated. Your prompts might include: What professional knowledge and values are relevant for this experience? How does it apply to this situation? Why was I feeling......... before, during, after the event? Why do I think.........? Where do my views come from?

Conclusion

At this stage your task is to consider all of the information gathered from the previous stages to help you achieve a new perspective, insight or awareness. Your prompts might include: How does my analysis change how I view this experience? What have I learned about my practice knowledge, skills and values? What have I learned about myself?

Action plan

Having reached your conclusions, your task at this stage is to plan how you will adapt or change aspects of your practice or address identified gaps in your knowledge or skills. Your prompts may include: What aspects of my practice will I retain? What needs to change? How will I do it? Who might assist me? What do I need to do now?

Having completed the reflective process you have now achieved new insight and awareness that will benefit your practice; but only when your future practice takes account of the learning achieved from the reflective process do you finally evidence your true skill as a reflective practitioner.

Activity

- Using Gibbs' Reflective Cycle, reflect on an event where you were dissatisfied with the outcome.

Holm and Stephenson's Reflective Activity (1994)

Holm and Stephenson have created a reflective framework that provides you with a complete series of reflective questions to prompt your thinking and analysis of a chosen event.

- What was my role in this situation?
- Did I feel comfortable or uncomfortable? Why?
- What action did I take?
- How did I and others act?
- Was it appropriate?
- Did I expect anything different to happen? What? Why?
- What knowledge from theory or research can I apply to this situation?
- What broader issues – for example, ethical, political or social – arise from this situation?
- What do I think about these broader issues?
- Do I feel I have learned anything new about myself?
- Has it changed my thinking in any way?
- How could I have improved the situation for myself or the service user?
- What can I change in the future?

This activity is designed to help you reflect retrospectively on an experience, but with some minor changes to the questions asked, it could also aid reflection prior to an event.

Crisp, Green Lister and Dutton (2005): Critical Incident Analysis (CIA) Framework

Available at: http://www.iriss.org.uk/resources/new-assessment-methods-evaluation-innovative-method-assessment-critical-incident-analysis.

The CIA is structured in such a way that it guides you through a process of critical reflection. The 'critical' aspect of the CIA refers more to the 'critical' or 'questioning' nature of the task, rather than a feature of the incident being used for reflection. It is possible that routine events, with positive and negative outcomes, can contribute 'critical' new insight or understandings that will inform your professional development;

so it is not necessary for you to look for the dramatic to find learning opportunities, or make good use of this reflective tool.

One of the key strengths of this tool is that it has the ability to enable learners to widen the reflective process by exploring Backward: Inward: Outward: Forward, as suggested by Seidel and Blythe (1996) and discussed in Chapter 3. This widening of the reflective process ensures that all of the key components that contribute to professional practice can be explored simultaneously, allowing you to experience a much fuller picture of your own practice by drawing attention to your integration of theory with practice, emotional self-awareness, ability to manage ethical dilemmas, collaborative skills and anti-oppressive practice.

The critical incident analysis framework

1 Account of the incident

What happened, where and when? Who was involved? What was your role/involvement in the incident? What was the context of this incident – e.g. previous involvement of yourself or another from this agency with this client/client group? What was the purpose and focus of your contact/intervention at this point?

2 Initial response to the incident

What were your thoughts and feelings at the time of this incident? What were the responses of other key individuals? If not known, what do you think these might have been?

3 Issues and dilemmas highlighted by this incident

What practice dilemmas were identified as a result of this incident? What are the values and ethical issues which are highlighted by this incident? Are there implications for interdisciplinary and/or inter-agency collaborations which you have identified as a result of this incident?

4 Learning

What have you learned, e.g. about yourself, relationships with others, the social work task, organizational policies and procedures? Which theory (or theories) has (or might have) helped develop your understanding about some aspects of this incident? What research has (or might have) helped develop your understanding about some aspect of this incident? How might an understanding of the legislative, organizational and policy contexts explain some aspects associated with this incident? What future learning needs have you identified as a result of this incident? How might this be achieved?

5 Outcomes

What were the outcomes of this incident for the various participants? Are there ways in which this incident has led (or might lead) to changes in how you think, feel or act in particular situations? What are your thoughts and feelings now about this incident?

You now have five tools to help you begin to actively engage in the process of reflection. The structures provided by these frameworks also allow you to create a more formal source of evidence of your reflective abilities for others who are involved in either the support or assessment of your learning and development. These tools lend themselves to thinking, questioning, analysing and evaluating, but the outcomes they achieve are considerably strengthened when you record your responses to each stage in the process. By capturing your responses on paper you build a picture of what you 'know' and begin to uncover what informs your 'knowing'. Creating this record can go a long way to helping you make links and connections that enable a new perspective to be achieved. The following chapter will focus on the significance of reflective writing in more detail.

Summary

This chapter has provided an introduction to reflective tools that can help you to develop your confidence and competence in the reflective process and encourage you to integrate reflective practice in your working routines. Reflective practice is an ongoing, lifelong commitment that relies on professional motivation, an openness to ongoing learning and a desire to deliver high-quality practice. These crucial features underpin the commitment that reflective practitioners display as they struggle to overcome hurdles such as lack of time, lack of confidence or non-reflective working environments.

Investing time and effort to develop your knowledge, understanding and application of reflective practice during your time as a learner will enable you to achieve a level of competence and confidence that you will carry with you into your professional career and provide you with the resources necessary to overcome some of the more common obstacles you are likely to face. Your allocated 'learning' time is invaluable as it increases the likelihood of you developing skilled reflective 'habits' and progressing to become an effective reflective practitioner who has already experienced the true worth of reflective practice (Thompson and Thompson, 2008a; Thompson and Thompson, 2008b; Taylor, 2010) and are committed to ensuring it remains an integral part of your practice routines.

6 Reflective writing

During their professional education and training learners will be expected to develop competence in a variety of styles of writing. Within higher education institutions (HEIs) written communication, such as essays or written exams, are a significant part of the learning experience as they provide a source of evidence that conveys a learner's ability to fulfil academic criteria, such as the acquisition of professional knowledge and understanding, and the successful achievement of professional standards, as outlined in the national occupation standards (TOPPS, 2002; SSSC, 2003). Qualifying professional education and training programmes also include the crucial element of assessed practice experiences where a social worker in training will be given opportunities to develop their skills in other forms of writing directly relevant to social work practice, such as the wide range of recording and reporting that form a major part of social work's role and responsibilities.

While there are differences in the style of writing used to complete an academic essay or compile a professional report, they do share some common principles and skills. Both require the writer to demonstrate an ability to accurately convey concrete, factual, information, an ability to utilize professional knowledge to aid understanding, and an ability to reach an informed conclusion or appropriate decision for future action.

To achieve professional standards learners are also required to develop the capacity and competence to manage, and be accountable for, their own practice, achieved in part through the development of their skills as reflective practitioners (TOPPS, 2002; SSSC, 2003; SSSC, 2008). As previously discussed in Chapters 2 and 3, critical reflection facilitates professional accountability by offering a process that encourages an ongoing examination of practice, a commitment to adapt and modify behaviour in light of experiences, and a recognition that ongoing professional development must be pursued if quality services are to be maintained.

To ensure professional standards are met, qualifying and post-qualifying professional courses are designed to ensure that learners have a range of assessed and non-assessed opportunities to provide evidence of their developing skills and competence as reflective practitioners, some of which will require written accounts that demonstrate the outcome of their reflections and capture their progress towards becoming a reflective practitioner. These written accounts may include specific reflective academic assignments, reflective tasks set by practice teachers (field educators) or a course requirement to maintain an ongoing written account or portfolio that documents the personal learning achieved as a result of a learner's reflective journey over time.

Reflective writing is a skill, and as with other forms of academic or professional writing it generally has to be learned. Your stage of learning – first/final-year undergraduate or postgraduate – and the level of reflection you have achieved will also influence the quality and depth of your written reflective accounts. Acquiring relevant knowledge and understanding, being prepared to persevere, and ongoing practice will result in you producing accomplished, written, critical, reflective accounts over time.

In Chapter 5, you were provided with a range of tools and techniques that facilitate the reflective process, helping you to think about 'how to' reflect. The aim of this chapter is to focus specifically on the development of your reflective writing skills so that you can effectively document the outcomes of these reflections, for yourself and others. If you are to commit your thoughts to paper, it is important that you begin the process with a clear sense of the purpose, challenges and professional benefits of reflective writing which will allow you to recognize the value and unique contribution reflective writing can make to standards of practice and ongoing professional development, not only during your professional training, but throughout your professional career. Having outlined 'why' you should engage in reflective writing, the chapter will offer practical guidance on 'what' and 'how' to write, thereby allowing you to further enhance the learning achieved from asking reflective questions. The chapter will conclude with some practical considerations which, if applied, will ensure you can maximize the effectiveness of your reflective records.

Activity

Before we begin, take a moment to note your current position.

- How would you assess your current levels of reflective writing skills on a scale of 1 to 5? (1 being poor, 5 being very good)
- What do you find most rewarding/challenging about reflective writing?
- What is the purpose of the reflective tasks you have written to date?
- How might you benefit from completing these tasks?

Purpose, challenges and benefits

Your current experience of reflective tasks may be associated with fulfilling course requirements or evidencing achievement of professional standards. But it is also accurate to say that the completion of these reflective tasks provides you with an opportunity to develop skills that will positively influence your ongoing professional development.

The key purpose of reflective writing is to further enhance the outcomes of your reflections, resulting in an increase in the quality and depth of the learning achieved from retrospectively critically examining your experiences (Moon, 2006; Knott and Scragg, 2007; Bolton, 2010).

By committing your knowledge, thoughts, feelings and actions to paper, you create a space in which to listen to and communicate with your 'self' (Brockbank and

McGill, 2007; Bolton, 2010). These written personal reflective conversations allow you to express and explore your experiences in greater depth by capturing relevant information that may have remained beneath the surface and out of reach if you were thinking alone or talking to others (Holly 1989; Rolfe et al., 2001) enabling you to extract important areas of learning before it is lost to you (Brockbank and McGill, 2007). Bolton argued that reflective writing was different from talking as it 'enables the writer to make contact with thoughts and ideas they did not know they had' (2001: 117), revisit forgotten memories, acquire new understandings and recognize connections.

Written reflective accounts provide you with your own 'footprints on the page' (Bolton, 2010: 106), creating a visual record of your current thinking, awareness, knowledge and learning that can be revisited and reconsidered in the future. This visual record of learning, if maintained over time, also demonstrates ongoing development as a reflective practitioner, acknowledges progress, recognizes skills and strengths and provides material that can act as a self-assessment tool. All of this can offer a positive contribution to learners' developing professional confidence.

Unlike other forms of academic or professional writing, reflective writing requires you to write in the first person singular, 'I'. Committing your thoughts, feelings and actions to paper in this way can be extremely enlightening, but for learners who are beginning their reflective journey, and focused on the successful achievement of academic milestones, it can be a cause of some anxiety and discomfort, particularly when you are expected to produce written accounts for others. This reaction is understandable as your written reflective accounts can highlight vulnerabilities, errors and prejudices, exposing aspects of yourself and your practice, which you may or may not have been aware of, for scrutiny by yourself and others. It is, however, this scrutinizing of 'how' you practise that allows you to maintain your professional competence, and therefore finding the motivation to explore those things that challenge you is an important part of the developmental process. When you recognize that this process is a valuable part of the ongoing leaning that sustains your professional development, you are likely to successfully shift your focus from personal considerations to a professional desire to deliver quality services to those in need.

The purpose of reflective writing is to enhance the outcome of your reflections, and therefore the account you transfer to paper is primarily for you. It is a personal space where you can stand back, question, explore your knowledge and feelings, and come to new understandings. You can create a 'safe' approach that works for you but still captures the content and outcomes of your reflections. You may prefer drawings, diagrams or free-flowing writing that does not have to be concerned with structure, grammar, spelling or punctuation.

It is initially difficult for learners to recognize the true value of this creative process and to accept that their written reflective accounts are rarely 'wrong' if they are an open and honest account of their thoughts, feelings and actions and lead to learning that can inform future practice and professional development. Sharing your written reflective accounts with others may feel a little uncomfortable, but you will be rewarded with an invaluable, objective, source of feedback that can inform the development of your reflective skills and your professional development. The reflective conversations you have with others will also play a significant part in helping you to achieve a new perspective in the most challenging aspects of practice, particularly in areas of personal development such as emotional awareness and managing ethical dilemmas. It is worth remembering that those who are supporting your ongoing development are likely to have experienced their own reflective journey and therefore have some insight into the challenges you are facing. Experiencing a 'safe' environment which encourages and supports your reflection can only be achieved, however, if you are open to the possibility and play a part in its creation.

Reflective writing makes a positive contribution to your professional competence and confidence as transferring your thoughts to paper helps to identify what you already know; it becomes your own 'private process of discovery' (Bolton, 2010: 105). The material captured in reflective documents is, however, more than a record of your knowledge; it becomes an account of a dialogue with yourself that enables new understandings to develop and greater clarity to be achieved.

Reflective writing enables you to unravel the muddle that can be experienced when you are trying to decide what is relevant from your existing knowledge, and the re-examination of what you know and feel that comes with the critical reflection of an incident. Sorting out what you know, considering new information, and attempting to adjust your previous knowledge in response to the new perspective offered by the reflective process can be a messy business, but one that leads to the development of your practice wisdom and confidence as a competent practitioner. The written account that facilitates this process may initially appear equally messy, but it is nonetheless rewarding as the well-documented benefits of this process confirm. Reflective writing enhances your ability to do the following:

- Manage uncertainty.
- Clarify thinking.
- Manage ethical dilemmas.
- Question everyday understandings and interpretations.
- Develop emotional self-awareness.
- Develop understanding of theory.
- Recognize and understand recurring patterns of behaviour in yourself and others.
- Make connections between past and present experiences.
- Explore areas you find difficult or unwilling to articulate.
- Formulate action plans.
- Identify professional development, progress and learning.

(Moon, 2004; Moon, 2006; Knott and Scragg, 2007; Fook, 2007b;
Thompson and Thompson, 2008b; Bolton, 2010)

Having considered the purpose, challenges and benefits of reflective writing, the following section will offer practical guidance that will enable you to write with purpose, overcome potential challenges, and experience the benefits this skill has to offer. Your reflective accounts are primarily for you. The process of compiling reflective accounts can be an empowering experience as it offers an opportunity for you to have control of your own learning through self-assessment and take action where needed to improve the quality and standard of your practice.

Writing reflectively

Before you begin to produce evidence for others, it is important that you initially allow yourself a means to write freely, without the restrictions of using appropriate written language or anxiety about what aspects of yourself you share with others. Your aim is to openly and honestly explore key practice experiences and create a record of your ongoing learning.

The most common vehicle used by learners to facilitate this free-flowing, ongoing, account of their reflections and learning is the 'learning or reflective journal'.

Learning journals are generally written in a language that is more conversational than other forms of writing (Moon, 2010) capturing a record of the personal reflective conversations you have with yourself. As the content is written in the first person singular this enables you to develop a 'greater understanding, and insight, of who "I" am and how "I" function as a practitioner' (Bolton, 2001: 157). This ongoing record captures your interpretation of an event at a given time (Taylor, 2010) and also provides you with a personal account that you can revisit and re-examine at a later date (Bolton, 2010). Allowing yourself some distance from the immediate impact of an experience creates further valuable opportunities for additional new perspectives to develop that may not have been possible at the time of the initial reflection.

Regularly recording these reflective conversations provides you with a 'map of your learning journey' (Brockbank and McGill, 2007: 337). At times it may appear to only represent your struggles and weaknesses, but as you unravel the answers to your reflective questions you will develop 'deeper levels of insight' (Holly, 1989: 14) and understanding that offers a positive way forward for your future practice. Creating this ongoing, personal, record of your reflections will also provide extensive examples of reflective material that you can adapt to fulfil the criteria of specific assessed or non-assessed written reflective tasks required during your course of study.

How you present your reflections in a learning journal is secondary to the content you choose to include. Bolton (2010: 105) argues that 'no one can get this writing wrong' as you recount your own interpretations of an experience when you write reflectively – reassuring news for those new to reflective writing. Trotter (1999a), however, highlights the dangers of being overly descriptive or overly critical of others. This acts as a reminder that even when personal or formal restrictions are lifted, it is crucial to maintain your reflective focus if your writing is to enhance the outcome of your reflections.

From descriptive to reflective writing

Those moments before you begin to write are usually filled with some trepidation. For those new to the art of reflective writing the initial response is to present 'the story' of their experience on paper, which results in a description of events rather than a reflective account.

Before beginning to write, plan your strategy: focus on the purpose of the task, identify the event you wish to reflect on and set clear objectives. For example:

- Critically analyse an experience in order to learn and develop future practice.
- Choose a section of an appropriate event rather than the whole experience.
- Identify appropriate reflective questions: maintain balance: identify future action.

Thinking and writing critically and analytically are professional skills that develop over time (Taylor, 2010; Forsyth Smith, 2010; Knott and Scragg, 2007), but in the early stages of your development reflective frameworks provide a valuable, temporary, alternative as they are designed specifically to encourage thinking beyond the facts of 'the story' and offer a practical structure that leads to the exploration, questioning and challenging of what you know.

What you 'know' may be more extensive than you first realize when you consider the multiple components that may contribute to professional practice. Creating a spidergram of potential knowledge may help you to focus your thinking and identify knowledge that is relevant for your specific reflection and chosen experience. An example of a spidergram has been provided to get you started; all of the components identified may not be relevant for each reflective process.

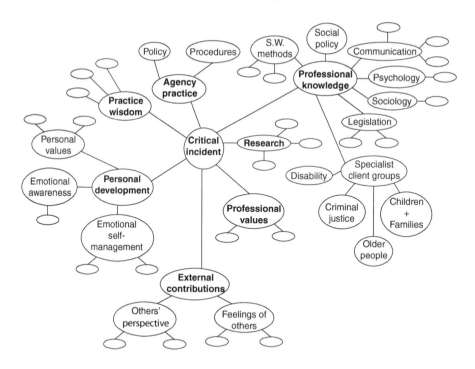

Having identified relevant knowledge – personal and professional – your next step is to ask reflective questions, such as those outlined in Chapter 5, that examine your current thinking and open up the possibility of developing a new perspective. An example of your writing during this process might read: *During .... I thought/I felt .... This might be because of/explained by .... My knowledge tells me that ....I now realize that .... My professional values expect me to...... ....but .... is making this difficult for me to achieve. I still need to .... I can achieve this by ....*

It is also important to ensure your reflective accounts maintain a balance between the positive and negative aspects of an experience, highlighting what went well, your strengths, your growing application of knowledge and values in practice, as well as your difficulties and concerns. A great deal of constructive learning can be extracted from experiences that had a positive outcome, allowing you to consolidate and confirm the development of your knowledge and understanding and increasing the likelihood of transferring your learning into new practice situations.

Reflective practice identifies change which has the potential to transform practice, so it is vital that you conclude with some thoughts on how you may adapt your thinking or practice as a result of the learning achieved through the reflective process.

Having considered features that inform the process of reflective writing, such as relevant knowledge, appropriate questions, balance and forward thinking, the following activity offers you an opportunity to consider examples of written accounts in order to further develop your understanding.

Activity

– Two accounts of the same event are provided for you.

Read Account 1: The seminar

This week I attended my first social work seminar group meeting. I've been looking forward to the social work module as it feels more relevant to the job than some of the other modules on the course seem to be.

Although the seminars will usually link to the topic discussed at the previous social work lecture, this week was about everyone in the group getting to know each other and being told how the seminar group will work.

I think it's good to have a chance to go into smaller groups to talk about the lecture topic as you have a chance to ask questions and iron out bits that perhaps haven't been clear in the lecture. There are 12 students and a tutor in the group, which seems an ok size to work in.

The tutor introduced herself and started by explaining the purpose of today's seminar. She then started by giving us an 'ice breaker' exercise to get us talking to each other. We were supposed to chat to every member of the group, but she didn't give us enough time for that so I only managed to speak to nine people. It was good to get a chance to speak to new people, but I would have liked more time for a proper chat.

I think I'm the only one in the group who has worked long-term in social care services. A couple of others have done voluntary work, and some have worked for about a year; but there are some in the group who have no experience of care work at all. It made me feel really old, but I'm glad I've got the experience of working in residential care. It must be hard coming in to train for something you've not really done as a job; but then again, the youngsters will find doing the essays easier than me, I guess.

After we had talked to each other the tutor asked us to introduce the person sitting next to us to the wider group, giving a little information about them. I suddenly remembered this exercise was used at selection interviews to show how good a listener you were. If this was a test, I think the tutor should have given us better instructions to start with. Anyway, I think my listening skills are fine, and the man next to me, Allan, lived in my area so I remembered our chat and was able to introduce him well enough.

After the 'ice breaker' the tutor told us what would be covered over the term, gave us information on the topic of each seminar meeting, and told us what reading we had to do before each session. I think my communication skills and interviewing skills are ok, but I'm not sure if 'role-play' exercises are of great value as everyone knows it's not real. I'm a little apprehensive about being videoed as I hate to hear or see myself on camera, but everyone else seemed to be equally worried about that bit.

In the final part of the seminar the tutor asked us to work in groups of four to come up with our preferred group ground rules so the group could become a safe, positive, environment to work in. I was able to contribute my thoughts to the small group and others agreed with me. The group asked me to feed back our thoughts to the big group. From all of the groups' ideas we had to make a group decision about which rules we thought were most important and that everyone would commit to. I was first to talk as the group were being very quiet, but then others joined in and we managed to agree five rules for the group: confidentiality, preparing for each sessions, active participation, valuing each other's contribution and being non-judgemental. I think that it's good to have a basis for our work together, but I'm not sure how we will deal with occasions when the rules are broken. The tutor says we are responsible for our working environment so I guess we have to sort it out ourselves.

I'm looking forward to next week's seminar and to getting started on the work.

Activity

Your thoughts on Account 1: The seminar
- Make a note of your thoughts on how it is written and highlight any areas you think are reflective.

Now read Account 2: The seminar

Account 2: The seminar
During my first social work seminar group I think I've achieved the goal set by the tutor: I now have a clearer sense of what's going to be expected of me and know the topic for each session so that I can prepare in advance. I was able to introduce myself and get to know a few of my fellow students, and I feel I contributed to the process of identifying our group ground rules.

I was looking forward to this module and went into the group feeling quite confident because of my work experience before coming on the course. Some of the content for this term is familiar to me because of attending in-service training courses run by my employer. I have practised and improved my use of questions, paraphrasing and listening skills in practice as a result of the knowledge I gained from previous training and believe my communication skills have developed over time. I've always shown respect for the service users I worked with, am aware of the importance of being non-judgemental, and understand why professional values are important in practice.

When I thought about the ground rules exercise we had completed I realized that I hadn't shown group members the same respect; instead I tried to take control of the situation because I felt irritated by the lack of information or direction offered by the tutor and frustrated by the group's lack of participation.

I don't see myself as a controlling person and it's uncomfortable to think I behaved like this. This new situation is so different from what I'm used to and, if I'm honest, being a student just leaves me feeling deskilled and dependent rather than feeling confident and relied upon by others. Having worked in the same team for a long time it's scary to think people I don't know are going to influence my learning and performance and others might decide I'm not good enough. Even being in a university feels unnatural as I see myself as a very practical person, and my last experience of education seems like a long time ago and I didn't do well. In practice situations I will at least have my previous experience to guide me, but I'm at a loss to think how I might successfully put together an essay.

I think my irritation and frustration in this seminar were because I thought I might do well in this module and it hasn't turned out the way I expected. I now realize that being a student is scary and my anxiety about others influencing my ability to get things right and being judged on my performance led me to try to take control of the situation and portray myself as more confident and knowledgeable than I feel, or maybe am. Instead of respecting others in the group I've dismissed the value of their contributions.

If I'm going to be able to fulfil the ground rules we've agreed in the group, I need to be aware of what's happening to me. I need to take the time to get to know my fellow students, talk less, be open to learning from their experiences and prepared to share my anxieties as well as my experiences.

I came to university to achieve a professional qualification, and although I was anxious about the academic work I don't think I'd considered how difficult the change would be. Somehow I need to accept that I won't get everything right and try to learn from the mistakes I make. When the time comes to submit essays, I need to look for resources and support that can initially help me achieve a successful outcome and draw on the general skills I've developed at work, such as time management, to help me plan and prepare for the academic assignments.

Activity

Your thoughts on Account 2: The seminar
Now make a note of your thoughts on how this account is written and highlight any areas you think are reflective.

Account 1 presents a narrative account of an event from an individual's perspective. Account 2 provides the reader with a sense of the writer looking back at an uncomfortable experience with the purpose of trying to understand her thoughts, feelings and actions. It provides an open and honest account of the outcome of her reflections, which have involved questioning and challenging herself before arriving at a new perspective about herself and accepting that some personal underlying issues may continue to influence her learning and development.

This activity highlights the differences between descriptive and reflective writing. You may have already recognized the changes that occurred in the content of these two accounts – a definite shift in what is communicated and how it is conveyed.

Activity

– Identify the changes that have occurred in the writing between Accounts 1 and 2.

Moon (2004) suggests descriptive writing can be avoided and reflective writing achieved by including the following shifts in the information being communicated:

- Moving from no questions to questions and responding to questions.
- Acknowledging emotional influences and exploring their impact on perceptions.
- Conveying a sense of 'standing back' from the event.
- Progression from self-questioning to challenging your own ideas.
- Recognition of the relevance of prior experiences.
- Taking others' views into account.
- A review of personal reflective processes.

Having captured a range of reflective examples in your learning journal, being alert to the dangers of descriptive writing and having a checklist to help you maintain a reflective focus to your writing, you are now well prepared to provide evidence of your skills and development as a reflective practitioner to others.

Purposeful reflection

Academic reflective assignments and tasks have a clear purpose and are designed around specific criteria that require learners to provide evidence of their ability to utilize reflective knowledge and skills to achieve a greater depth to their understanding of professional knowledge and/or values. These written reflective accounts require you to demonstrate your understanding of the application of professional knowledge and values in practice and, over time, enhance your ability to critique 'what you know' and 'do', conveying your developing 'professional knowing' (Schön, 1983) or 'practice wisdom' (Thompson, 2009; Humphrey, 2011), as discussed in Chapter 3.

It is important that you familiarize yourself with the assignment criteria and follow guidelines offered by your course of study, including the acceptability of writing in the first person singular. The development of emotional awareness is not usually required in academic assignments, but may be the subject of specific developmental reflective tasks in practice. It is not necessary to choose a major event as your subject example to successfully achieve the required criteria, so try not to identify a 'complex' experience as you will spend too much energy outlining the details of the event, leaving less time for you to convey the outcomes of your reflections.

The learning evidenced in this type of 'purposeful reflection' (Ryan, 2011: 101) will be influenced by the level of reflection achieved. For example, 'technical' reflection, which draws solely on theory to examine skills, provide explanations or solutions; 'practical' reflection, which draws on both tacit and formal theory to develop insight and identify potential areas of change; and 'critical' reflection, which incorporates aspects of the previous two levels, but has the added features of challenging underlying assumptions and questioning the application of professional values in practice (Van Manen, 1977), as summarized by Ruch (2000) in Chapter 3. As you progress and develop deeper levels of reflection, your written accounts will reveal evidence of associated reflective skills, such as analysis, evaluation and self-awareness being applied. These deeper levels of reflection are achieved by asking reflective questions that explore 'How?' or 'Why?', to assist your analysis of an event; and your evaluations can be informed by asking 'How well...?', to explore the effectiveness of your actions or your application of knowledge or values in practice, and 'What about...?', to allow you to examine different perspectives or consider wider pertinent issues. Questioning 'What does this mean for my future practice?' enables you to complete the reflective process and convey how the learning achieved can inform future practice and professional development (Brown and Rutter, 2009).

Social workers in training are expected to have demonstrated competence as critically reflective practitioners by the completion of their professional education and training. Reflective frameworks, such as Critical Incident Analysis, enable you to begin to shape and develop your critical thinking skills, but the feedback and guidance you receive from others who are supporting your professional development will play a significant part in the successful achievement of this highest level of reflection (Trotter, 1999a; Bolton, 2010).

You may find Moon's (2004) 'A Generic Framework for Reflective Writing', which describes levels of reflective writing, and Moon's (2007) 'Framework for Critical Thinking and its Representations', which describes levels of critical thinking, useful additional resources to inform your thinking in this area. Copies of these, and other useful learning materials, can be freely obtained from: www.cemp.ac.uk/people/jennymoon.php.

Critical thinkers are open-minded, prepared to relinquish personal beliefs, and open to change (Jones, 2009). These qualities do have to be acquired and tested in practice, but the process of critical reflection facilitates their development by encouraging challenging reflective questions to be asked. You may also find it useful to revisit the discussion on critical reflection provided in Chapter 3.

ıve to critically reflective writing

.e additional 'critical' dimension in your written reflective accounts you ıre that, where relevant, you are asking yourself reflective questions that:

- Challenge existing social, political and cultural norms (Ruch, 2000; Fook, 2007b; Thompson and Thompson, 2008b), your own and others' assumptions and beliefs (Jones, 2009), power differentials (Fook, 2007b), and theoretical perspectives (Thompson and Thompson, 2008b).
2 Generate awareness of personal feelings and their impact on how you interact with others and explore different or competing perspectives of your own or others (Fook, 2007b; Thompson and Thompson, 2008b).
3 Inform your understanding of how theory informs practice, how issues link and connect, and how there is rarely one 'right' approach or perspective (Thompson and Thompson, 2008b; Forsyth Smith, 2010).

Although the technical knowledge that would normally be necessary in purposeful reflective accounts has not been included, Account 3: The seminar has been provided as an example of how a critical dimension can be added to your ongoing reflective accounts.

Account 3: The seminar

In this week's seminar we talked about professional values and how our personal values and beliefs influenced how we interpret situations. It made me think about my first seminar and consider what assumptions I'd made about other group members. I'd assumed that a tutor's role would be to guide and direct our learning but now realize this doesn't always mean telling us what to do; it can also involve occasions where they accept that we are all different and give us time and space to develop at our own pace. The idea of being responsible for my own learning is uncomfortable, but I need to recognize that tutors will not only assess my performance – they will also support my development. And so my first step to access this support is to ask for what I need.

I also realize that I believed that young people wouldn't have life or work experiences that were valuable for my learning and that their age gave them an academic advantage. These assumptions and beliefs are based on generalizations and are unhelpful if I'm to recognize the value of each member of my group as an individual and for the contribution they might make to my own learning. Without questioning these assumptions I'm less likely to be open to what others have to offer or recognize other people's concerns.

Looking back at these early seminars has been helpful as it has made me recognize how difficult it is to make changes in your life and how the anxiety I felt influenced how I had behaved. I believe that my previous life and work experiences will be a useful foundation for my learning, and I'm happy to share these experiences with others, but also look forward to being more open to learn from others' experiences. I think my wish to do well on the course and learn how to be a competent professional is both a strength and weakness. The positive side has given me the motivation to question myself, to acknowledge my anxiety and fears, and begin to accept my limitations in this new environment and look out for other occasions where my feelings might drive my actions so that I can stop and think about how I can respond more appropriately. This awareness will also help me to think differently about service users'/carers' behaviour and look more closely at what might be behind their actions.

Asking appropriate reflective questions generates the material you need to successfully address the criteria in your purposeful reflective assignment. In the previous section, Moon's (2004) thoughts on how to 'shift' from descriptive to reflective writing were considered; but to take the final step, and convey the deep learning you have achieved as a result of critical reflection, Cottrell (2003) suggests a further 'shift' in focus is required. Cottrell (2003) argues that your discussion should also include:

- Identifying the significance of the event.
- An evaluation of strengths and weaknesses.
- An examination of why theory is relevant or suitable.
- Questioning the suitability or appropriateness of an approach or method.
- An exploration of the relevance of potential links between issues or information.
- Identifying learning achieved, and an explanation of how this will influence future practice.

Activity

- Identify the 'shift' in the information conveyed in Account 3 that provides this critical dimension.

By challenging, evaluating, questioning, analysing and understanding your own and others' existing norms and practices, you increase the likelihood of successfully conveying your ability to deliver ethical practice and identify potential areas of change that can transform existing practice.

This final section draws together a range of practical considerations that can positively influence the effectiveness of your reflective records.

Practical considerations

When compiling your ongoing reflective accounts you must ensure the rules of confidentiality are vigorously applied, even if the content is written solely for your own use.

If your course requires you to maintain a learning journal, or similar ongoing record of your reflections over time, you may initially wish to consider using a looseleaf folder or ring binder to store your free-flowing accounts separately from the adapted accounts that you are comfortable to share with others.

The discussion so far has focused on written rather than typed accounts as the written word is thought to be easier for learners (Taylor, 2010) due to the association of typed communication with academic or practice work (Bolton, 2010) rather than for yourself. If, however, you communicate more freely in typed form, then maintain the system that is most comfortable for you.

It is crucial that you develop the habit of writing regular reflective accounts – for example, in a learning journal (Knott and Scragg, 2007; Thompson and Thompson, 2008b; Bolton, 2010) if you are to accumulate a valuable record of your learning and development and create a resource which contributes to the completion of more formal reflective assignments or tasks.

You should ensure you date all entries and try to avoid deleting or changing your entries once written (Taylor, 2010; Bolton, 2010). The content may feel a little uncomfortable at times, but you will lose your sense of progress if you have no reminder of where you came from.

Before beginning to write, find yourself some private space in which to think without interruption (Bolton, 2010). It is believed that our most creative thinking occurs when we are tired (Brockbank and McGill, 2007; Bolton, 2010). If possible, try to begin your reflections reasonably soon after the incident, but find a time that allows you a little distance from the emotional context without being too far removed that you have lost the details or impact of the experience (Brockbank and McGill, 2007; Thompson and Thompson, 2008b; Bolton, 2010; Taylor, 2010).

Summary

This chapter has outlined the key purpose, challenges and benefits of reflective writing in order to highlight the valuable contribution this aspect of the reflective process offers to the quality of your practice and ongoing professional development.

The act of writing reflectively accesses information that exists below the immediate consciousness, enabling it to resurface and inform new insights and understandings.

The initial discomfort experienced by those new to the task is acknowledged, but you are encouraged to persevere and take a risk so that you can benefit from deeper learning and enhance your reflective skills through the support and guidance offered by others.

The chapter considered two types of written reflective accounts – free-flowing and purposeful – each written for different audiences and purpose, but both contributing to the depth of learning achieved as a result of your reflections. Maintaining an ongoing learning journal has been recommended to encourage you to write freely, for yourself, creating a personal record of your progress and development. This resource will also capture valuable material which can be adapted for the 'purposeful' reflective assignments and tasks that will evidence your learning to others, demonstrating your achievement of professional competence as a reflective practitioner.

Finally, the focus of this chapter has been to offer guidance on 'what' and 'how' to write reflectively, including practical suggestions that will encourage positive habits. Being clear about the purpose of your task, utilizing reflective frameworks to initially guide your thinking and analysis, and incorporating a reflective 'shift' (Cottrell, 2003; Moon, 2004) in the content of your accounts provides a strategy that ensures overly descriptive writing is avoided and critical reflection can be developed and conveyed.

7   Reflecting in and on practice

This chapter is written specifically for social workers in training and those responsible for supervising part, or all of, the practice-based elements of students' professional education and training.

Learning in practice is a central feature of professional education and training as it provides crucial opportunities and evidence of students' development of professional competence and provides the foundations for the development of their professional identity and confidence. For qualified practitioners, ongoing learning in practice is also an important feature of post-qualifying education and training (GSCC, 2005; SSSC, 2008) and a requirement for continued professional registration. Although the discussion will be constructed around students engaged in qualifying education and training programmes, the content is also directly intended for those practitioners involved in facilitating the learning of others. This is in recognition of the invaluable learning opportunity this activity offers practitioners' development, either as part of post-qualifying education and training or an ongoing commitment to maintain and improve their own standards of practice.

The chapter does not intend to address the wide topic of practice learning but instead will concentrate on the key elements necessary to create a learning environment that encourages and supports the reflective process and provides an accurate account of students' achievements and professional development.

Reflecting in and on practice is necessary for students to achieve professional competence and confidence, and those facilitating the learning of others need to create a positive environment that enables students to learn from their experiences and empowers them to become active participants in their own developmental journey, while simultaneously ensuring professional standards are maintained.

The chapter will initially focus on four crucial elements that enable this complex process to become an enriching and stimulating experience for all participants – an environment founded on interpersonal interactions which enable reflective dialogues to generate growth and development, enhance self-assessment skills and demonstrate progress and development to others. The areas considered necessary to create such an environment include: developing learning partnerships, redefining power relations, the adult learning experience, and effective supervision.

The assessment of students' performance is a central feature of the placement function and the accuracy and reliability of the assessment outcomes are enhanced when the assessment process becomes an integral part of existing learning partnerships. The purpose, processes and principles that guide competent assessments are outlined to establish a shared understanding of this central feature of the placement experience and to encourage active participation for all participants.

The final section of the chapter will explore the concept of reflexivity and consider its value for supervisors committed to monitoring and evaluating the quality of their own performance.

Terminology

The honours degree in social work introduced a wide range of terminology to describe practice-based learning (practice learning, field education, practice placement) and those who manage, supervise and assess a student's practice during practice-based experiences (practice teacher, practice educator, practice assessor). For the purpose of this chapter, however, the following terms will be used to denote these key features of practice-based teaching and learning:

> *Student:* refers to an individual undertaking a professional education and training programme.
> *Placement:* refers to the practice setting where a student is based as part of their professional education and training programme.
> *Supervisor:* refers to an individual who undertakes a supportive, educational or managerial function with a student during their placement experience.

Setting the scene: learning in practice

Social work has a long history of integrating academic and practice components into the design of professional education and training. The current honours degree in social work requires students to complete 200 days of direct practice, have experience of working with two different service user groups, and an opportunity to fulfil statutory roles and responsibilities, before a professional qualification can be achieved (Department of Health, 2002; SSSC, 2003).

The significance of practice-based learning has increased in recent years due to employers' need to employ social workers who are competent and confident professionals 'able to do the job, able to work collaboratively, skilled and knowledgeable and responsible for their own continuous developmental needs' (Parker, 2010; 57).

Practice-based experiences allow students to gain direct experience of working within a professional culture, to function within an organization, and develop their understanding of the application of professional knowledge, skills and values in practice. Undertaking this direct experience of practice is crucial for professional growth and development, but it cannot be achieved without the cooperation and partnerships that exist between university social work programmes and local and national statutory, voluntary and independent service providers who provide placement opportunities for social work students.

These partnerships aim to be mutually beneficial as universities gain access to the practice-based experiences necessary for students to complete their professional qualification and service providers gain students who contribute to the work of a team, stimulate learning in others, and enable prospective employers to play a part in ensuring they have a bank of knowledgeable and skilled practitioners to recruit in the future.

The organizational context in which a student is placed plays an important part in the quality and effectiveness of their learning experience; but it is their integration with the team of practitioners they will be working with and learning from that initially has the most significant impact on a student's experience. While an individual is likely to facilitate, manage and coordinate the placement overall, implementing an 'integrated approach' to placement experiences ensures a team involvement in the teaching, learning and assessment of a student's practice (Bruce, Cree and Gillies, 2005). This team approach allows the responsibilities associated with student placements to be shared and is less onerous than previous approaches (Practice Learning Taskforce, 2003; Bruce, Cree and Gillies, 2005); but it also enables a wide range of practitioners to be actively engaged in the future development of the profession and embraces the Social Care Institute for Excellence (SCIE) (Kearney, 2003) and Social Work Services Inspectorate's (SWSI) (2004) principle that 'practice learning is everybody's business'.

Durkin and Shergill's (2000) research acknowledged that having a student on placement brings additional responsibilities for already busy practitioners, but clearly highlights that team involvement in the organization, planning, implementation and evaluation of placements is crucial for a successful outcome and considerably reduces the likelihood of problems arising during the student's practice experience. Implementing a team approach to students' practice experiences provides benefits for all parties involved; a student has access to a wealth of knowledge and expertise which adds depth and breadth to their learning, the supervisor/facilitator has a collaborative and reflective working experience, the team benefit from the integration of fresh ideas and reflective opportunities (Bruce and Lishman, 2004), and service users experience 'more effective ways of working' (Durkin and Shergill, 2000: 173).

Participating in the teaching, learning and assessment of students also offers practitioners an important opportunity to reflect on their own social work practice (Walker, Crawford and Parker, 2008) and on their role as 'enablers': contributing to professional registration requirements (GSCC, 2005) and in keeping with the professional code of practice (GSCC, 2002a; SSSC, 2005). Practitioners who are open and committed to continuous learning will utilize their own reflections to strengthen the learning environment being created for students by demonstrating good practice and acknowledging the shared learning and development opportunities that occur during a placement (Ringel, 2001).

For those working in learning organizations the concept of continuous learning is embedded in an organizational culture which regards all work experiences as potential opportunities for new learning (Kerka, 1995). Reflective practice would be actively encouraged in this working environment, with structures in place – such as practitioner forums or peer supervision – to enable staff to explore their practice and share their learning, each investing in and gaining from the learning culture of the workplace. Students offer a significant contribution to these working environments as they bring with them a wealth of up-to-date research and theory, a fresh look at service provision, and an interest in reflective conversations with colleagues about their practice.

When students enter the workplace they rely on organizations and teams to have effective systems in place to guide and support them while they manage the challenges of practice. The role of supervisor, and the supervisory process, are a crucial source of this support and guidance and determine the outcome of the placement (Walker et al., 2008). Students have a responsibility to ensure they fully engage with the learning process offered by the placement agency, but the quality and effectiveness of the learning they achieve will be significantly influenced by supervisors' ability to identify a range of relevant teaching and learning opportunities that specifically address students' professional and personal developmental needs. The teaching element provided by supervisors is important for students to acquire information that allows them to function within the agency and develop a sense of 'how to' deliver practice effectively. The learning elements, however, will involve much more than 'simply absorbing knowledge or modelling skills' (Parker, 2010: 55) observed in others, but instead arise when students are encouraged and supported to reflect on their own practice experiences within the supervisory process. This reflection 'in' and 'on' practice facilitates a deeper understanding that leads to a change in 'how to' practise more effectively that would be lost to the less 'thoughtful' practitioner (Yelloly and Henkel, 1995).

Regular supervision provides the forum that enables the social (communication and collaboration), cognitive (developing knowledge and skills) and emotional (acknowledging feelings and motivations) dimension of learning (Illeris, 2003) to be fulfilled, allowing students to grow and develop professional competence and confidence.

Placements do not purely provide students with practice experiences; they also function as a means of assessing students' ability to achieve professional competence in stages throughout their professional education and training. Supervisors' decisions should be based on credible sources of evidence, and students should be active participants in the evidence-gathering process that will determine the outcome of the placement.

The following sections will explore four key elements that make an important contribution to the quality of the learning environment created for students: developing learning partnerships, redefining power relations, the adult learning experience, and effective supervision.

Before progressing, just take a moment to contemplate your 'ideal' learning environment.

Activity
– Describe your ideal learning environment. – Consider why these features are important to you.

Preparing the way

Reflection is the key to learning from experience, and the depth of reflection achieved can be enhanced when the process is facilitated by 'significant others' (Bolton, 2010). Reflective activities that involve sharing thoughts, feelings and behaviours with others require a learning environment that is supportive, non-judgemental and safe (Tsui, 2005). For those contributing to the learning of others, constructing the foundations of a positive learning environment begins prior to a student arriving in the agency. Using an 'integrated approach', the planning, preparation and negotiation with colleagues, other professionals, service users and carers are intended to clarify opportunities, roles, responsibilities and expectations, and agree systems for monitoring and evaluating the placement package.

Supervisors will benefit from time to reflect on their personal approach to supervision, their methods of assessment, their feedback skills, and also familiarize themselves with the assessment criteria and general requirements of their partner university. Practical considerations, such as workspace, phone, internet/intranet access and employee identification, can be difficult to guarantee in some agencies, but these components are crucial for a student's integration into the organization and ability to function as a team member. The outcome of this process provides the basis for an agency profile that captures the essence of the agency and general placement package (Beverley and Worsley, 2007) that can be offered to a student, allowing them to prepare for the placement and feel secure that their learning needs will be met by the setting in which they will placed. This early preparation not only begins to shape a learning environment that empowers a student, but also allows each participant to recognize the role they play in supporting the learning of others and their contribution to maintaining professional standards that will ensure quality services in the future.

The planning process continues once the student has been matched to the agency and met with their supervisor and team. A personal profile, provided by the student, enables the supervisor to familiarize themselves with a student's learning needs, their previous work, life and educational experiences, expectations and current commitments, all of which can usefully inform early negotiation and decisions that will shape the placement to 'fit' the student.

This initial process normally culminates in documents such as a learning agreement/supervision contract, with a practice curriculum either integrated with or an addendum to the main learning agreement, which should be completed jointly by the supervisor and student in the early stages of the placement (Beverley and Worsley, 2007; Walker et al., 2008; Parker, 2010).

Developing learning partnerships

With a secure foundation in place and the learning agreement in progress the supervisor and student are then able to focus on creating the learning partnership that will enable both parties to grow and develop their competence and confidence over the duration of the placement – the student in their capacity as a competent social worker and the supervisor in their capacity to facilitate the learning of others.

Beverley and Worsley (2007: 19) define the learning partnership as a 'constructive relationship centred on enabling learning where partners manage the process of utilizing learning opportunities for reflection, development and the evaluation and evidencing of professional practice'.

The significance of this supervisory relationship is well documented in practice-based, experiential learning literature (Beverley and Worsley, 2007; Walker et al., 2008; Hawkins and Shohet, 2009). The literature review undertaken by Pehrson, Panos, Larson and Cox (2009) offers a range of useful insights into the crucial influence this relationship has on students' practice, supervisors' assessments, and ultimately the well-being of service users. According to Behling, Curtis and Foster (1982) 'impediments' in this relationship negatively influenced learning: Fox (1998) argued the relationship influenced the potential outcome of the placement, determining a student's ability to develop professional knowledge and skills and integrate professional values; and Bogo (1998) and Fox (1998) suggested that students initially modelled their relationships with service users on the relationship experienced with supervisors (cited in Pehrson et al., 2009: 73–4). Ultimately, the effectiveness of the supervisory relationship impacts on the quality of services offered to service users (Overholster, 2004), but Lefevre's (2005) study also suggested that students believed their relationship with supervisors impacted on the effectiveness and accuracy of the supervisor's assessment.

As student and supervisor begin their new working relationship they each bring preconceived ideas based on their own previous experiences of supervision, teaching, learning and assessment. It is vital that their early communication should explore these past experiences to consider how they may influence the current relationship and agree effective responses that may prevent problems from arising (Walker et al., 2008; Pehrson et al., 2009).

Activity

In one word, capture the essence of your last experience of:

- being supervised
- learning a new skill
- having your performance evaluated.

How might these experiences influence your new educational relationships?

Points of tension are not uncommon in supervisory relationships. What is important is that 'both parties actively take responsibility to monitor their behaviour so that they can individually and jointly develop strategies that will bring the relationship back on track' (Hawkins and Shohet, 2009: 4).

Effective interpersonal communication is crucial to the development of all successful relationships. The task of the supervisor is to help a student 'feel valued, understood and safe' (Hawkins and Shohet, 2009: 50). But the supervisor's role is not just to reassure or quality assure students' practice; it is also to encourage students to explore personal dilemmas and their emotional responses to practice events (Hawkins and Shohet, 2009). Without a 'safe' and 'trustworthy' relationship it is more difficult for students to effectively share their reflections or develop strategies to manage tensions experienced between personal and professional values. A supervisor's response to information shared by a student will have a major influence on their working relationship. By demonstrating genuineness and empathy, supervisors can reassure students that their views are heard, understood, accepted and valuable to the learning process, thereby laying the foundations for a safe environment to explore personal challenges. Developing trust takes time and 'has to be earned' (Cousins, 2004: 177); but placements are time limited, so the pace for developing the relationship needs to be accelerated to accommodate such constraints. Supervisors who are empathic, open to students making mistakes, encourage the sharing of concerns and are comfortable sharing their own thoughts and feelings will be more successful in their attempts to create a trusting environment that is conducive to sharing and learning (Schulman, 1982, cited in Beverley and Worsley, 2007).

Despite a supervisor's best efforts, an effective learning partnership will not develop without a student accepting their share of responsibility for the effectiveness of the supervisory process and relationship (Tsui, 2005). Students are required to demonstrate their commitment to the placement and the interpersonal relationship with their supervisor by: actively engaging with agreed learning opportunities, participating in the supervisory process by sharing their thoughts and views, being open to the constructive feedback offered, monitoring and evaluating their own performance, identifying learning gaps, negotiating opportunities to address developmental needs, and providing supervisors with credible evidence of their progress and development of professional competence (Inskipp and Proctor, 1993; Walker et al., 2008; Hawkins and Shohet, 2009).

A flexible, individualized and open approach is needed (Walker et al., 2008) from both parties if a learning partnership, where power and responsibility are shared and a supportive and nurturing environment that aims to facilitate professional development is to be achieved (Lefevre, 2005).

The student–supervisor relationship begins with a clear imbalance of power which, if unaddressed, will negatively impact on the effectiveness of the working partnership and ultimately, the outcome of the placement. It is important for supervisors to consider how best to redefine the power relations within the supervisory relationship and for students to take on board the new opportunities and responsibilities that arise from this sharing of power and authority.

Redefining power relations

Power and authority are 'inescapable' realities of the supervisory relationship (Shardlow and Doel, 1996: 115). Kadushin and Harkness (2002) described 'authority' as 'the right to control others' and 'power' as 'the ability to do so' (cited in Walker et al., 2008:

114). Supervisors have delegated organizational and professional authority inherent in their role due to their responsibility to ensure professional standards of practice are maintained and organizational functions are fulfilled. Brown and Bourne (1996) argued that supervisors have both formal and informal power: formal power derived from their position as supervisors and informal power derived from their professional skills, expertise and their structural position in society.

Characteristics such as 'race, gender, age, sexual orientation and (dis)ability are structurally determined identities that can result in informal power being embedded in an individual's identity' (Brown and Bourne, 1996: 39). Examples where structural disadvantage may become a feature of the supervisory relationship would include matching a 'mature' student with a 'young' supervisor, a male student with a female supervisor, or a black student with a white supervisor. Where potential differences such as these are present it is important for supervisors and students to maintain an open dialogue that explores how potential differences may influence personal perceptions, action, and the dynamic of the student–supervisor relationship.

Despite practitioners being familiar with the power and authority inherent in the social work role, many supervisors struggle to redefine the power relations within the supervisory relationship due to the challenges that come with the dual responsibility of supporting students' development and assessing performance. Avoiding this relational dynamic is likely to result in avoidance behaviour that will stifle any attempts to appropriately manage the issue or look for ways to empower students when circumstances allow. Avoiding the issue is also confusing for students who are very clear about the considerable authority and power inherent in the supervisor's role and diminishes their opportunity to develop effective strategies to manage the power/authority inherent in the social work role.

Tsui (2005) suggests that power games develop when participants are struggling to work in partnership, want to gain some advantage, or are having difficulty managing their own and others' authority and power. Within the supervisory relationship both parties have equal ability to initiate and maintain this type of unhelpful behaviour. Hawkins and Shohet (2009: 53) and Beverley and Worsley (2007: 99) identify potential power games played by individuals who prefer to abdicate power with excuses such as 'Poor me', where avoidance and cancellations are explained by how difficult life is and how busy they are. Other games associated with the manipulation of power include playing 'Mother/father/supervisor knows best', where the approach taken displays patronizing/parental/childlike behaviour which disempowers others by holding on to power, or avoids engaging with power/authority issues. Students may also play games such as 'Treat me don't beat me' (Kadushin, 1992) in the hope of drawing supervisors into the 'helper' role, changing the dynamics of the supervisory relationship, which allows the student to abdicate responsibility for partnership working or becoming a self-directed learner.

It is unrealistic to suggest that the power imbalance between supervisor and student can, or should be, eradicated as this would deny the existence of the organizational and professional authority and power inherent in the supervisor's role. Supervisors can, however, begin to redefine the power imbalances early in the relationship by providing students with information, identifying resources, and seeking students' opinions (Beverley and Worsley, 2007) which empower them to take the initiative and work more autonomously. To maintain an environment that empowers students a supervisor should:

- Display an open and honest relationship that engages in a dialogue of the potential influence of power differentials in the relationship and make decisions about what can be shared and how it will be put into practice.
- Emphasize how professional values underpin beliefs regarding the equal value of each individual and apply this in practice.
- Readdress power imbalances by identifying support networks that offer additional support outwith the placement for students who are structurally disadvantaged.

(Walker et al., 2008: 116)

Both students and supervisors should, individually and jointly, critically reflect on the impact of their thoughts, feelings and behaviour within the working relationship as a means of evaluating the learning partnership and identifying positive strategies that address motivational factors that result in unhelpful game playing.

Adult learning theory and theories of learning offer some useful insights that may positively influence the development of new educational relationships by recognizing the value of previous experiences and identifying strategies that facilitate the adult learning process.

The adult learning experience

Achieving professional competence involves a personal developmental journey for each individual student due to the influence of their own previous educational, work and life experiences (Miflin, 2004). Knowles' (1984: 1990) theory of adult learning has had a strong influence on our understanding of the adult learning process, and in turn has informed the design of learning environments in higher education and in placements. Knowles (1990) believed that adults' learning is goal driven, and as a result they learn more effectively when they are actively involved in the learning process and recognize how learning activities enable them to achieve their identified goals. Knowles (1984) also argued that an individual's previous experiences were an asset to the learning process as they provided a foundation for exploring current perspectives and the subsequent identification of future goals or learning needs. Given the uniqueness of each individual's previous experiences Knowles (1990) suggested that adult learners benefited from having a range of teaching and learning opportunities available to avoid disadvantaging the outcome of their learning and allowing strengths to be recognized.

Within the context of placements this perspective comes alive when we consider how focused participants become on students' achievement of learning outcomes, and how often supervision sessions evolve around problem-solving activities as supervisors enable students to find their way to becoming professionally competent.

Although placement learning outcomes will inform the basis of a supervisor's choice of learning opportunities and provide the criteria for the assessment process, it is important for supervisors to make sure students' learning does not become overly task-orientated or driven by 'tick-box' processes. Supervisors can reassure students how placement learning outcomes will be addressed by clearly demonstrating the links between identified learning opportunities, the methods of assessment being applied, and specific learning outcomes. Enabling students to appreciate the purpose of learning activities and encouraging them to take control of their own learning by participating in the evaluation of their own performance allows students to recognize that evidence of their successful achievements and development will be demonstrated by a developmental process that revolves around the interaction between delivering services and reflecting on their experiences to improve future practice.

Our understanding of the 'learning' process is also informed by a range of psychological theories. The *behavioural school* argues that learning can be achieved from observing and modelling the actions of others, and highlights the importance of goal setting, the use of positive reinforcement and regular feedback to stimulate new actions. The *cognitive school* regards learning as developmental, with new learning being constructed through a process of examining the subject/experience against what is already known. Reflective conversations with others, ongoing feedback and goal setting are also regarded as crucial components of this learning process. The *humanist school* believes the individual is the most important element in the learning process – a unique individual who is motivated to grow and develop through a process of self-awareness, with facilitators charged with creating an empowering environment where it is possible for them to proactively achieve their goal. And finally, the *experiential school* centres learning around reflection and the process of revisiting personal experiences to examine, question and explore new possibilities that can enable positive change to occur (Beverley and Worsley, 2007; Walker et al., 2008; Parker, 2010).

While the *experiential school* fits more directly with the basis of professional education and training, each of these models can usefully enhance student's learning by informing the learning activities, such as those outlined in Chapter 5, and the reflective conversations that form part of the supervisory process. These reflective activities can be designed to capture the principles of each model of learning by encouraging students to examine and analyse the thoughts, feelings and behaviours experienced in practice events, resulting in new perspectives or awareness which can transform future practice.

Kolb's (1984) Experiential Learning Cycle presented learning as a continuous cycle, facilitated by reflecting on experiences. This approach to learning later generated some suggestion that individuals develop preferred learning styles, at different times for different situations (Walker et al., 2008). Honey and Mumford's (2000) Learning Styles Inventory is offered to students in many universities as a first step to exploring their own preferred style of learning and to encourage the development of new skills and approaches that would enable a greater depth of learning to be achieved in the future. Honey and Mumford suggest that individuals may prefer to be 'active', 'reflective', 'theorizing' or 'experimental' learners (Walker et al., 2008: 45): that is to say, learning by doing, standing back and exploring the situation, looking to knowledge for explanations or experimenting with new actions. Kolb (1984) believed that learning was enhanced when individuals could skilfully integrate all four modes of learning, thereby integrating all the component parts necessary for the reflective process. An individual's preferred learning style is not fixed; it will alter over time and be influenced by the learning environment they experience and their reflective abilities. By encouraging and supporting students to engage in a range of reflective activities, supervisors create opportunities for students to develop the full range of skills necessary to achieve the deep learning that can transform future practice as they become more competent reflective practitioners.

It is important that both students and supervisors have some awareness of their own, present, preferred style of learning if they are to make the most of the learning potential of the placement (Lucas, 2002). For example, those who prefer to learn 'by doing' may find reflective approaches to learning more challenging, but with support will expand the depth of their knowledge and understanding of 'what', 'how' and 'why' they think, feel and act in practice as they do. This can be an important factor in students' development and the assessment process, particularly if a supervisor and student have polarized preferred approaches: one preferring active learning – 'jump in and see' approach, the other preferring a more reflective – 'stand back and think' approach, which can result in supervisors misunderstanding students' behaviour and progress (Beverley and Worsley, 2007).

Activity
– Identify your current 'preferred' and 'less developed' learning styles.

There are occasions when a student coming into placement has specific additional learning needs. This is an area that often causes concern for both students and supervisors: students are concerned about how their needs will be perceived by the supervisor, and the agency and supervisors are concerned about how they can ensure sufficient support and learning opportunities are available for the duration of the placement.

It is important that the pre-placement meeting, involving the tutor, student and supervisor, is used to discuss the detail of a student's requirements, and agreement reached regarding how these needs will be addressed during the placement. The university may have undertaken an initial assessment of the student's learning needs and have a support plan in place. While this assessment is confidential, a student has to make an informed decision about what information the supervisor and agency require to know if they are to create a positive learning environment. Once information is shared, the agency is then able to fulfil their legal responsibility to address and manage the identified needs as they would for other employees. Despite the anxiety that may be associated with sharing sensitive personal information with a 'significant' individual at the beginning of a new relationship, it is in a student's best interest to do so. Not only does this begin an open and honest working relationship, it also enables the supervisor to create learning experiences that 'fit' with each student's needs and allows a partnership to develop that shares responsibility to identify issues and find solutions.

A student's previous life, work and educational experiences can enhance the learning achieved in placement, but it can also result in students developing personal barriers that inhibit effective learning. Previous negative supervisory relationships or established negative mental processes (see Chapter 4) can have a significant influence on each new learning environment and student–supervisor relationships. The uncertainty over levels of competence and assessment anxiety that comes with each new placement experience can result in students struggling to function effectively in an environment in which they feel vulnerable. High levels of anxiety inhibit learning, and vulnerability can result in a range of unhelpful behavioural responses (see Chapter 4). Gilbert and Evans (2000) suggested that students may attempt to compensate for the negative emotions they experience by displaying behaviours such as:

- Magnifying their own shortcomings.
- Abdicating power to supervisors.
- Overemphasizing the supervisor's assessment function.
- Finding it difficult to accept support.

Left unexplored, such behaviours may have a serious impact on a student's learning and the supervisory relationship. It is important, therefore, that students' reflections on previous learning experiences should also include some examination of their behavioural responses in times of stress so that they can share this insight and identify potential challenges with a new supervisor and work together to develop appropriate ways forward.

Activity

- Describe how you previously responded to stressful learning experiences.
- What would help your new learning experiences to be less stressful?
- How might this be achieved?

The reflective process is central to the successful achievement of professional development and it is therefore crucial that supervisors embed a range of reflective activities within supervision so that they can support students to extract learning from their practice experiences (Beatty, 2003). It is not uncommon for students to find reflection challenging, but providing structured reflective activities and offering guidance through regular feedback, students can develop and enhance their reflective skills and experience the benefits of reflective practice (Roberts, 2009). Given the time, space and support to examine and discover their professional 'self' students are more likely to become self-directed learners who can diagnose their own learning needs, identify appropriate opportunities to meet these needs, and learn how to evaluate the outcomes of their learning (Knowles, 1990).

Supervision provides the central platform for students' learning, development and critical evaluation of performance and therefore the supervisory process can usefully be guided by the principles of 'learning' theories to ensure this learning environment is conducive to adult learning. While there is currently no common approach to supervision in operation, the following section aims to highlight significant key features that ensure supervisors can provide a supportive, flexible environment that values previous experiences, acknowledges strengths, enables students to function effectively and grow in confidence. To be effective, this environment should be structured around a developmental approach to learning. It therefore needs to be able to adapt to the changing needs of each student, integrate regular feedback to guide students' future learning, and be underpinned by professional values that ensure professional boundaries and confidentiality create a safe environment in which to explore the emotional context of practice and the developing professional self.

Effective supervision

A variety of patterns of supervision currently exist across the United Kingdom such as the traditional, one-to-one student–supervisor partnership, individual placement facilitators coordinating multiple 'task-specific' supervisors for one student, or a combination of individual and group supervision sessions (Bruce et al., 2005). It is beyond the scope of this chapter to sufficiently address all of these variations, so the content will focus specifically on those occasions when a student has individual time with a designated supervisor.

The primary purpose of professional supervision is to ensure that service users and carers receive high-quality services (Walker et al., 2008; Hawkins and Shohet, 2009; Parker, 2010). However, the model of supervision offered to students is designed to extend beyond case management by embracing the principles of developmental approaches to learning where professional competence is achieved in stages during the life of each placement and over the duration of a student's professional education and training (Brown and Bourne, 1996; Hawkins and Shohet, 2009). The supervisory process aims to support and assess students' learning and development, within an environment that enables professional competence to be developed through practice experiences and reflective practice, in order to gain a deeper understanding of the application of professional knowledge, skills and values in practice, construct their professional identity and develop professional confidence.

To create such an environment, in addition to developing an encouraging and empathic working relationship, a supervisor must integrate the managerial, educative and supportive functions of the supervisory process (Kadushin, 1992) to ensure the quality of practice delivered by students meets professional and organizational standards (Parker, 2010), allow professional skills, understanding and ability to develop (Stratham, 2004), and enable students to effectively manage the emotional context of practice (Niklasson, 2006).

The managerial or qualitative (Hawkins and Shohet, 2009) function is primarily to monitor and evaluate a student's ability to perform the roles and responsibilities of a social worker to a professional standard and comply with organizational policy and procedures. Casework offers students the opportunity to reflect on the quality of their practice against clear professional standards and procedures outlined by their supervisor, examine their application of technical knowledge and evaluate their interpersonal skills. Through reflective conversations or activities, students can develop their understanding of 'good enough' practice, begin to identify value-related dilemmas and explore their professional identity.

The educational – also known as developmental (Hawkins and Shohet, 2009) – function of supervision requires supervisors to create teaching and learning opportunities that enable students to develop the knowledge, skills and values necessary to effectively fulfil their professional roles and responsibilities. Supervisors fulfil their teaching responsibilities by providing information that relates specifically to their area of practice – such as organizational policy and procedures, legislation, assessment frameworks, evidence-based methods of intervention and local or national resources – and teach students how this knowledge should be applied in practice. By offering students the opportunity to observe supervisors' or colleagues' practice, students are also taught 'how to' carry out agency tasks effectively, providing them with models of good practice which they can replicate in their own practice (Tsui, 2005; Walker et al., 2008).

A supervisor facilitates student learning by encouraging and supporting the development of critical reflective skills that will enable them to question theory, assumptions and values and begin to recognize how perceptions and experiences shape what is 'known' and understood (Dalrymple and Burke, 2006). Reflective frameworks and tasks offer students the opportunity to engage in a reflective process that enables them to critically evaluate their own performance in their team/organization/with other professionals, analyse the application of their professional knowledge and skills, and discover their 'professional self' by examining how their personal values and biographies influence their practice (Dalrymple and Burke, 2006).

Feedback received from supervisors and significant others, such as colleagues, service users and carers, significantly contributes to students' learning and development (Walker et al., 2008; Parker, 2010). The purpose of feedback is to enhance students' learning and enable progress and development; but to be effective, supervisors require relevant communication skills and students need to understand the purpose and significance of the information being conveyed. Supervisors should ensure that their feedback enhances rather than damages a student's self-esteem by conveying information in a way that enables a student to hear and accept the comments offered. In return, a student has to overcome the anxiety that comes from the assessment process and recognize that the feedback offered is a necessary part of the developmental process and exists to enable them to achieve professional competence and a successful outcome to the placement.

The term 'feedback' may not do justice to the process that facilitates development and empowers students as it merely implies a backward-looking process. A supervisor is not only sharing their view of a student's performance; they are also aiming to enable a student to compare their own performance with the 'ideal' so that they can develop self-assessment skills and begin to identify opportunities to address their own learning needs. For this to be achieved, the process requires looking backwards and guiding future action: feedback and 'feed-forward'. Supervisors should discuss identified strengths and areas of development with a student to ensure the feedback has been heard and understood before jointly clarifying how learning needs can be addressed.

Beverley and Worsley (2007: 137) provide one of a number of useful mnemonics that help ensure constructive feedback is provided: SCORE.

Specific: Feedback should identify specific examples of what has been done well and areas for improvement. Areas of development should also include comment on how progress can be achieved.

Clear: Avoid vague comments or generalities. Ensure that areas of identified change are realistic and encourage students to contribute their thoughts on strategies for change.

Owned: Supervisors should present their personal views clearly by using 'I' statements and ensure follow-up discussions with a student to expand their understanding.

Regular: Feedback should be an ongoing part of the developmental process and should be provided soon after the practice task is completed. Time should be made available to offer initial verbal comments and initiate discussions with a student to alleviate anxiety and capture student's self-assessment. These discussions should be followed up with a timely written summary that provides a more detailed account for students to digest.

Even-handed: Feedback should present a balance of strengths and areas of development and avoid 'but' or 'although' statements as these diminish any prior positive comments.

Supervisors have expressed concern that students will become complacent or misinterpret the context of ongoing encouraging feedback, with some believing that criticism or anxiety focuses student's learning (Evans, 1999; Rogers, 2001; Beverley and Worsley, 2007). In my experience, criticism or lack of encouragement results in students feeling demotivated and disempowered. Students who receive regular, skilled, feedback are able to transfer 'good enough' practice to new situations, develop their self-assessment skills and acquire professional confidence.

Activity
– Reflect on your previous experience of receiving/giving feedback and identify three positive and three negative features that were important to you.
– What challenges do you face when receiving feedback, and why?
– How might you overcome these barriers?

The supportive – also known as the resourcing (Hawkins and Shohet, 2009) – function of supervision aims to respond to the emotional needs of students by enabling them to reflect on the emotional challenges experienced in practice and supporting them to identify, acknowledge and effectively manage their emotional responses to practice events or the learning process. This element of supervision plays a crucial role in enabling students to resolve professional dilemmas and begin to develop their capacity to integrate professional values in practice by reflecting on the origins of their personal values, analysing the implications of their beliefs and identifying strategies to manage personal and professional tension.

According to Tsui (2005), emotional support is a unique function of social work supervision and exists to ensure that practitioners can develop and maintain adequate levels of self-care. Placements will raise a number of emotional issues for students, either as a result of their own personal biographies or as a result of encountering events they have not personally experienced such as death, disability or violence. A significant part of students' development as competent professionals will involve personal reflection to develop new levels of emotional self-awareness and emotional self-management (see Chapter 4). Students will, however, need clear direction on the value and legitimacy of sharing their emotional responses to practice events (Barlow and Hall, 2007) and require supervisors to draw on their own emotional intelligence to effectively engage and respond to students' emotional needs and offering them examples of good practice to model with others in the future.

To avoid supervision becoming a 'therapy' session the supervisory process should ensure professional boundaries are maintained. Students and supervisors should agree that the personal issues discussed within supervision are restricted to areas generated from the work undertaken or areas affecting working relationships, including the supervisory relationship (Hawkins and Shohet, 2009; Parker, 2010; Humphrey, 2011). In the event of students requiring additional support, supervisors should help students to access appropriate professional services. When discussing the boundaries that shape the supervisory relationship, it is also crucial to ensure students have a clear understanding of the limitations of confidentiality that will apply during the placement. As a developing professional, each placement forms part of a wider assessment process which continues throughout a student's education and training. A consequence of this wider assessment process is that all material provided by students and/or witnessed by supervisors can be accessed by other stakeholders at later stages in the student's developmental journey. Supervisors also need to be very clear about their responsibilities to ensure the care and protection of service users and clarify circumstances in which information gathered during the placement may need to be shared more widely – for example, with university staff in the event of concerns about the student or their practice. To ensure clarity and transparency, a written statement confirming the agreed boundaries for the relationships and outlining the limitations of confidentiality should be included in the placement agreement/contract completed at the beginning of the placement.

These complementary functions of supervision aim to empower students to become active participants in their own learning by embedding reflective conversations within the supervisory process. To maximize student's learning, supervisors should ensure that all three functions are integrated within each formal supervision session where possible. This may prove challenging as supervisors are presented with a range of situations, such as occasions when tension exists between functions, levels of student competence, supervisors' preference or time constraints, which may result in one function dominating at the expense of the other two. Other than the beginning of a placement, when students require more case management time and the supervisory relationship is in its infancy, supervisors should ensure that a balance is maintained between monitoring service delivery and addressing students' developmental and emotional needs if supervision is to have an effective impact on students' practice and professional development.

The opportunity to grow and develop professional competence through 'real-life' activities, in an environment that encourages and supports learning, is invaluable, but students also have to demonstrate their achievement of professional standards in practice in order for supervisors to reach a decision about the outcome of the placement. The assessment of students' performance is an essential feature of the placement experience (Coulshed and Orme, 2006; Walker et al., 2008) and having a positive environment in which to learn ensures this assessment provides a more accurate and valid account of students' achievements and capacity to 'do the job' (Tsui, 2005). To enable the assessment process to become an integral part of existing learning partnerships the following section will outline the purpose, processes and principles of assessment to inform the basis of students' and supervisors' shared understanding of this central aspect of the placement experience.

Assessing performance

Undertaking assessments is an integral part of the social work role, and the knowledge, skills and values necessary to complete this function are transferable to the task of assessing students' performance during placements. Assessment criteria provide the parameters within which an assessment is constructed and these vary depending on the purpose of the assessment process. The purpose of student assessment may differ from standard professional assessments but the process of gathering information from a range of sources, weighing up the evidence gathered, and drawing conclusions that will form the basis of future action apply equally to both practice and student assessment. The following discussion provides the context for student assessment, outlining the specific features of the assessment process and highlighting the principles that inform competent practice.

The purpose of assessment

The purpose of the assessment is to establish whether or not a student has successfully achieved the specific learning outcomes/assessment criteria identified for the placement to a level appropriate to their stage of learning. Students are expected to become active participants in the assessment process and have a responsibility to provide supervisors with evidence of their ongoing progress and development throughout the duration of the placement.

Supervisors are responsible for the collection and evaluation of a range of sources of evidence that demonstrate students' performance and are required to record their decisions about students' progress, development and future learning needs at agreed points in the placement – for example, at the midway point and/or the end of the placement (Walker et al., 2008). Supervisors are accountable for their assessment decisions and need to ensure their judgements are credible, informed by an under-standing of the assessment process, underpinned by the principles of assessment, and can be substantiated to others (Coulshed and Orme, 2006).

The assessment process

An effective assessment process requires both student and supervisor to be clear about the learning outcomes for the placement and have an understanding of the level of performance expected from a student at their stage of learning (Evans, 1999). Each university will usually provide supervisors with information regarding the assessment criteria for the placement, identify the required core standards (TOPPS, 2002; SSSC, 2003) and learning outcomes to be assessed, and offer guidance on the levels of com-petence expected. Supervisors and students are often concerned with what constitutes 'good enough' practice, so if uncertainty exists, it is prudent to ask for guidance directly from the student's university.

In general terms a student's knowledge, skills and ability to integrate professional values will be determined by their course curriculum and previous experiences of prac-tice or placements. University tutors' assessment and previous placement reports will contribute to the identification of students' learning needs at the beginning of each new placement, but students' own perspective of their previous learning achievements and learning needs are crucial when determining an agreed starting point for the assessment process. This contribution involves them in the assessment process from the beginning of the placement and will shape joint decisions regarding the identifica-tion of appropriate learning opportunities during the placement.

The developmental approach to professional competence creates a structure that encourages progression from the first to the final placement. The successful achieve-ment of foundation skills, such as interpersonal communication, can be transferred and enhanced in each placement. Whereas a student's ability to undertake informed assessments may initially be mechanistic and overly reliant on assessment frameworks, they should develop greater depth as their knowledge, understanding and reflective abilities improve. Each placement will present students with new challenges, both per-sonally and professionally, but managing uncertainty and identifying strategies that help them move forward should improve with the development of their new-found competence and confidence.

Once the learning outcomes and levels of performance are established, supervi-sors should ensure that a range of sources of evidence and methods of assessment are employed to provide valid evidence that will inform decisions regarding a stu-dent's performance (Evans, 1999). The supervisory process is a major contributor to the evidence-gathering process, but it is vital that additional evidence is gathered from external sources – such as feedback from colleagues, other professionals, service users and carers – to add credibility and fairness to the assessment process. Early planning and negotiation are necessary if supervisors are to equip these contributors with the necessary information that enables them to make an effective and valuable contribu-tion to the evidence-gathering process. It is useful to negotiate, identify and record specific learning outcomes that will be the focus of their contribution and agree learning opportunities that will facilitate this process: for example, service users who will have contact with a student should be asked if they wish to be involved in the student's assessment and, if agreeable, should be asked to comment on specific areas, agreed in advance, such as the student's ability to listen or convey respect, or timekeeping. This information can then be shared with students so that they are clear what is being assessed, when it is being assessed, and who is doing the assessing, rather than feeling 'under a microscope' for the entire duration of the placement. Feedback received from these participants should be shared with students in supervision and used to guide reflective conversations that can result in students adapting their actions.

Making decisions based on a range of sources of information strengthens the reliability of the process as it offers confirmation of students' achievements and highlights their ability to transfer learning from one situation to another. There will be occasions when the evidence gathered will provide conflicting points of view, and supervisors will have to evaluate each piece of information and decide on a course of action that will enable them to reconcile these different perspectives – for example, designing an activity that will offer students the opportunity to reflect on a specific aspect of practice, or undertaking relevant tasks that would target particular knowledge, skills or values.

Supervisors should also ensure a range of methods of assessment are available to inform the assessment process. Individual tasks and reflective activities are valuable sources of evidence of students' progress and development, but it is important to utilize students' strengths by allowing competence to be demonstrated in a variety of different ways – for example, use of video or audio clips to evidence the integration of professional values, visual presentations to convey knowledge and understanding, as well as the more traditional form of written tasks such as reflective accounts or direct observation of practice.

Students are engaged in a learning process, so these formative methods of assessment should enhance students' understanding and application of professional knowledge, skills and values. This process allows the outcome of the assessment activity to become part of a student's developmental journey as it identifies strengths, highlights areas of development and builds confidence (Light, Cox and Calkins, 2009). It is important that students and supervisors agree a model of understanding of reflection from which they can both work to establish clear expectations and acknowledge the value attached to students' reflective accounts by identifying the part they will play in the assessment process (Issitt, 1999).

When designing formative assessment activities, as with the negotiations with external contributors, it is useful to specifically identify the learning outcomes that will be addressed so that students can recognize how the activity relates to their final goal and supervisors can maintain a timeline and record of a student's performance that will inform the final, summative assessment of the placement.

Suskie (2004) argued that good assessment activities should provide useful and accurate information that informs assessment decisions and protects the dignity of all those involved. Reflective activities, such as those outlined in Chapter 5, achieve this goal by inviting supervisors to experience events through students' eyes, 'illuminating what the self and others have experienced' (Raelin, 2002: 66), allowing students' abilities and weaknesses to surface, and encouraging reflective conversations that demonstrate students' achievement of new understandings and growing competence.

Assessment principles

The outcome of the assessment process has major consequences for all participants, but particularly for students. It is therefore crucial that the assessment process is rigorous, credible and accurately reflects students' current level of ability to perform the social work task. When identifying effective methods of assessment that will inform the assessment process, Evans (1999) suggests the following principles should be applied to ensure the methods chosen are fit for purpose:

Validity	Does the method adequately assess the required criteria?
Reliability	Does the method provide consistent results?
Practicability	Is the method easily administered?
Fairness	Does the method make reasonable demands on the student?
Usefulness	Does the method contribute to students' learning?

Student participation in the assessment process will enhance the quality of evidence available to supervisors and others, providing a more accurate account of their progress, development and competence (Lefevre, 2005; Coulshed and Orme, 2006). Students need to be motivated to take on this responsibility, but supervisors have a key role to play in empowering students to become active participants in the assessment process and encouraging the development of students' self-assessment skills through the process of reflecting on practice.

Nolan and Caldock (1996) suggested that students can be empowered to engage in the assessment process by 'good assessors' applying the following principles to their practice:

- Establish a suitable learning environment.
- Involve others in the assessment process.
- Provide students with information and clarification about the assessment process.
- Establish existing levels of knowledge and skill.
- Clarify assessment criteria with students.
- Agree the level of competence expected.
- Choose appropriate methods of assessment and discuss them with students.
- Encourage self-assessment through reflective activities.
- Seek out and affirm students' contributions.
- Be open-minded and prepared to learn.

Good assessment relies on good supervisory practice. This requires supervisors to have a clear grasp of the assessment criteria and expected level of performance, regular contact with their students and others involved in students' assessment, the ability to maintain a structure and focus for students' learning, a range of reliable methods of assessment available, a commitment to providing ongoing constructive feedback that facilitates learning, and systems in place to accurately record ongoing progress and development.

Activity

- Capture your hopes, fears and expectations for the next assessment process you encounter.
- How might you ensure your expectations are fulfilled and your fears reduced?

The significance of a supervisor's responsibility to facilitate students' learning and assess professional competence has been consistently emphasized, but how can supervisors be confident that their practice is 'good enough' to adequately fulfil this crucial role?

The final section of the chapter will consider the importance of supervisors embedding reflective approaches in their own practice and provide an outline of reflexive practice to facilitate supervisors' self-evaluations.

The reflexive supervisor

If supervisors are to effectively enable students to develop as competent, reflective practitioners they should lead by example and demonstrate the value of reflecting in and on practice by sharing their reflections with students. Engaging in reflective conversations, and commenting on students' reflective accounts, not only enhances students' reflective abilities (Roberts, 2009) but also provides supervisors with opportunities to examine their own application of knowledge, skills and values in practice in order to develop new understandings and enhance future practice. Sustaining placement relationships, managing the complexities within supervisory functions, empowering others, and exploring practice events and dilemmas with students create many challenges, but also offer numerous opportunities for supervisors to address the social, cognitive and emotional dimensions (Illeris, 2003) of their own learning and future development as a supervisor.

To competently fulfil their responsibilities to facilitate students' development, accurately assess students' performance and enhance their supervisory skills, it is important that supervisors engage in reflective activities that effectively evaluate their performance and ability in this role. Supervisors who create time and space to critically reflect on the supervisory process and interactions with students are able to explore and examine the potential influence of their own thoughts, feelings and behaviours and identify underlying assumptions that may be influencing the assessment process (Coulshed and Orme, 2006).

Reflexive practice offers a useful addition to a practitioner's reflective toolbox as it encourages the development of greater awareness of the underlying assumptions that influence the way we make sense of situations, particularly when individuals have the authority to use their professional discretion (D'Cruz, Gillingham and Melendez, 2007b), as is the case in student assessment. It is this high degree of self-awareness, role-awareness and awareness of the assumptions that inform our perception of situations that is a distinguishing feature of reflexive practitioners (Sheppard, 2007). This offers an important dimension to the reflective process as the outcome of students' assessment is influenced by supervisors' interpretation of the evidence gathered during the assessment process (Coulshed and Orme, 2006). Hawkins and Shohet (2009: 98) argued that supervisors need to be aware of the personal 'lens' through which they experience placement events, identifying the influence of 'one's own racial, cultural and gender biases and prejudices' that can shape interpretations and perceptions.

D'Cruz et al. (2007a) suggest that reflexive practitioners should:

- Critically review the knowledge that informs interpretations of situations.
- Question connections between structural power and interpersonal relationships.
- Explore personal emotional responses to events.

To practise applying reflexive approaches, take a moment to scrutinize what you 'know' and how you 'know' it and discover the 'lens' through which you currently make sense of placement situations.

Activity

- What preconceptions or assumptions do I have about students, supervisors, learning processes, power relations, assessment processes or individuals contributing to students' assessment?
- What knowledge has influenced these opinions?
- How am I feeling about my previous or current placement? Why might I be feeling this way?
- Do I use my power productively? If not, why not? How can I improve?
- How do my experiences contribute to my behaviour and/or the conclusions I reach?
- Is there another way of understanding this situation?

The outcome of such reflection can be uncomfortable, but it is preferable to 'be able to locate oneself in the picture and appreciate how one's "self" influences actions' (Fook, 2002) rather than having assessment decisions influenced by less conscious motivations. Unlike other reflective approaches, reflexivity is not so concerned with what has been done or influencing future practice; instead, it becomes a 'critical process of thinking about thinking' so that the new awareness achieved can result in a more 'rigorous' and ethical approach to practice in the present (Lam, Wong and Leung, 2007: 96).

To fully benefit from reflexive approaches practitioners should have a good knowledge and understanding of the reflective process and have experience of critically reflecting on their practice. Chapter 3 may offer a useful reminder of the theoretical foundations of 'reflection'. Achieving reflexivity enables supervisors to adapt current practice in direct response to the new insights achieved, ensuring greater reliability and fairness are embedded in the assessment process, and increasing supervisors' confidence in the decisions that inform their assessment outcomes and practice.

Summary

This chapter has outlined key aspects of the practice-based element of professional education and training, with particular focus on: the creation of a positive learning environment that ensures students can effectively learn and develop professional competence; acknowledgement of the purpose, process and principles that inform student assessment to facilitate a shared understanding that ensures an accurate account of students' achievements and professional standards of practice; and an exploration of reflexive approaches that enable supervisors to monitor and evaluate their own performance.

The knowledge provided aims to ensure that all participants involved in the practice-based elements of professional education and training can play an active part in a learning process that enhances their own professional development and the professional development of others.

8   Moving forward

The purpose of social work education and training is to provide teaching and learning opportunities that enable learners to achieve and absorb the knowledge, skills and values required of a professional social worker, to become part of the professional culture and facilitate the development of individuals' professional identity. Academic staff, learning peer groups, practice supervisors, agency colleagues, service users and carers will all contribute to this developmental journey, but each individual learner has the ultimate control and responsibility to determine the professional they become. Social workers, and those drawn to the profession, are generally motivated to provide quality services, but achieving this goal means embracing the principles of lifelong learning and embedding reflective practice in normal working routines.

The content of the book locates reflective practice at the heart of a competent and confident professional workforce, not only because it is a requirement of professional qualifying and post-qualifying education and training, but also in recognition of social workers' intentions to make a positive difference to people's lives. A desire to avoid the continual doubt and discomfort that can arise when managing the complexity and uncertainty inherent in social work practice is a strong motivator that encourages practitioners to seek solutions that can alleviate these negative emotions regardless of external rules and requirements. Adopting a reflective approach offers an attractive, albeit challenging, alternative as it allows practitioners to achieve the professional satisfaction and comfort that come from knowing that one's practice is informed by a process that acknowledges strengths, examines knowledge, highlights areas of development and facilitates personal well-being.

As a developing professional it is crucial that you begin the process of constructing your reflective knowledge and skills in order to enhance your learning and achieve the required levels of professional development by completing your initial professional education and training. The content of the book is designed to provide you with all the necessary building blocks to enable you to develop a good working knowledge of the reflective process. It also introduces you to a collection of practical tools that will facilitate and encourage you to reflect on your professional experiences, allowing you to develop your reflective skills and demonstrate your development as a reflective practitioner to others. The support and encouragement you will receive from others during your education and training are an important part of the development of your reflective knowledge and skills. These interactions provide crucial opportunities to achieve a greater depth of understanding and level of skill that can transform your practice and provide you with first-hand experience of the value of the reflective process that will strengthen your commitment to engage in ongoing professional development throughout your professional career.

The chapter will highlight key messages from each of the preceding chapters in order to capture the knowledge, understanding and skills you have available to inform your development as a reflective practitioner and enable you to move forward with confidence to take responsibility for the quality of your future practice and professional development.

At all levels of professional education and training there is a strong emphasis on the importance of professional development to achieve professional competence and to maintain and improve standards of professional performance. For those entering the profession, a lack of understanding of this terminology can delay progress and development as learners struggle to connect with this generic aspect of their professional education.

The intention of Chapter 2 was to return to basics and explore what lies behind these concepts. It outlined the responsibilities and external expectations that need to be fulfilled when you become a professional, offered a clear definition of professional performance, and provided an explanation of the concept of professional development so learners can understand the wider context of their professional education, training and practice and develop a clear sense of why reflective practice is central to the development of competent performance and how it facilitates ongoing learning and development.

The key message is that social work practice is about much more than just doing a job (Jones, 2009). When you achieve professional status you also inherit responsibilities and are required to fulfil a range of external expectations from organizations, such as professional bodies and employers, and those in receipt of services.

The public expect their professionals to have completed rigorous education and training that have been designed to ensure new practitioners are competent to undertake specific occupational functions to a standard that ensures the delivery of effective services. Professionals have a responsibility to make a positive contribution to the wellbeing of others, are accountable for their actions, and therefore require a commitment to continually evaluate their practice and improve their performance by learning from experiences.

The chapter argued that providing a professional service requires more than fulfilling occupational functions competently, and so you were introduced to the concept of professional performance which captures more accurately the qualities and characteristics that should underpin and guide the professional you become. Effective professional performance relies on each practitioner having a professional knowledge base that informs their practice, an approach to practice that is underpinned by common professional values, and a commitment to ongoing professional development.

The range of knowledge required for social workers to effectively fulfil society's needs was explored, highlighting the importance of incorporating service user/carer 'expert' views and identifying the conceptual, procedural and strategic (Cust, 1995) knowledge sources that inform practice. Having a shared set of professional values contributes to a collective professional identity and culture as it provides the foundations for the profession's aspirations and provides a framework on which to base 'good' practice. However, you were reminded that achieving the integration of professional values in practice requires an ongoing examination of the personal values that shape your interactions with others in order to recognize personal–professional tensions. Professional development was described as a process of ongoing self-assessment and a commitment to learn from your experiences. This process involves both exploring and challenging personal beliefs and being open to new perspectives, as well as standing back, analysing and reconsidering the application of your professional knowledge, skills and values.

To enable the profession to fulfil their responsibility to learn from experiences and enhance their performance requires a credible system that enables learning to be extracted from practice experiences and effectively incorporates the social, cognitive and emotional complexities that underpin professional practice. Reflective practice offers this system by providing a framework that is designed to facilitate professional development by examining personal influences, mental processes and emotional responses to practice events in order to identify strengths, highlight areas of development, and encourage change that can transform future practice.

If you are to embed reflective practice in your normal working routines, it is vital that you acquire a sound knowledge of the concept of reflection and an understanding of the reflective process that will facilitate your professional development.

In Chapter 3 you were provided with an overview of the theoretical basis of reflective practice and reflection as described by some of the original pioneers who provided the foundations for our current knowledge and understanding, and from contemporary writers who have contributed new perspectives to further inform our understanding.

The key messages offered by these writers provide a good basis from which to launch your development as a reflective practitioner. Firstly, it is important for you to recognize the distinction between reflection and reflective practice. Reflection describes the detailed thinking and analysing processes that allow you to achieve a new perspective, but this process on its own does not automatically improve the quality of your practice. It is only when the outcome of reflective thinking is used to effect change in your thoughts, feelings or action that reflective practice has been achieved and practice can be enhanced.

The reflective skills necessary for professional practice have to be learned, even by those who are 'naturally' reflective. By adopting a questioning approach to life and work, and being open to developing a greater level of self-awareness, reflective practice can be achieved over time, with ability and skill developing with practise and support. Your aim is to consciously engage in a process that intends to routinely examine 'What you do', 'How you did it' and 'Why that way?', so that you can extract learning from your practice experiences that will lead you to new understandings and enable you to continually construct and reconstruct what you 'know' and 'do' in light of your reflections. This is an ongoing process that is intended to become an integral part of your normal working routines, but it is important to remember that reflective practice is not intended to make practitioners feel bad about themselves; in fact the opposite is true, as reflective practitioners tend to be more confident because they routinely question, learn and adapt their practice. You may initially be drawn to reflective practice to help you process uncomfortable or challenging events; but do not overlook the benefits of reflecting on positive experiences as these allow you to identify professional strengths and build professional confidence, and are therefore equally valuable.

All of the writers referred to in Chapter 3 have made a significant contribution to our professional knowledge and understanding of reflective practice, but Seidel and Blythe's (1996) advice to look Backward – Inward – Outward – Forward effectively captures the essence of the reflective process. The depth of reflection you will achieve at each stage will develop in conjunction with your professional knowledge, values and skills, levels of emotional awareness and emotional self-management, awareness and management of social and cultural influences, and your willingness to capitalize on the reflective process to transform future thinking and action. Your goal is to become a critically reflective practitioner who seeks to transform their practice by questioning their internal mental processes and challenge existing social, political and cultural conditions that sustain inequality and disadvantage.

Learning and development is a personal journey, with individuals bringing their own social and cultural context to each new experience. Reflecting on the internal mental processes experienced as a result of your emotional response to practice events, and critically examining the influence of personal values and beliefs, are central to learning and a crucial feature of your professional development (Boud and Walker, 1998).

To inform this personal developmental journey, Chapter 4 provided you with an outline of emotional intelligence as a means of developing the skills necessary for you to acknowledge and manage your own emotions in practice and enhance your capacity to respond appropriately to the emotions of others. The central message from Chapter 4 is that emotional intelligence enables practitioners to take care of their own emotional well-being and the emotional well-being of others, identifying a clear link between your personal development and your professional performance.

Identifying, acknowledging and responding to the emotions of others are fundamental features of social work practice and crucial for the development of therapeutic relationships, but your capacity to respond appropriately will be determined by your ability to identify, acknowledge and regulate your own emotions. Recognizing that your own emotions can influence how you relate to others is challenging, but to do so empowers you to acquire knowledge and skills that will allow you to develop effective strategies that ensure you can take care of yourself and build effective therapeutic relationships that enable individuals to overcome their personal difficulties.

The chapter argues that emotionally intelligent individuals have the capacity to effectively regulate their own emotional responses and skilfully respond to the emotional needs of others due to their intrapersonal and interpersonal abilities. Given the relevance for practice, the chapter explored each of these elements in more detail to offer direction and focus for your development of the skills necessary to achieve these crucial abilities.

Achieving intrapersonal competence ensures you can recognize, acknowledge and manage your own emotions in practice, but this requires you to develop your emotional self-awareness, emotional understanding and emotional self-management. Reflection provides the framework and space to identify your feelings and discover/understand the source of the emotions being experienced. By 'tuning in' to your emotional response to practice events you acknowledge the validity of your feelings and can take action to support your own emotional well-being.

To be effective, the reflective process requires knowledge to inform the critical analysis of events and so you have been provided with additional knowledge on cognitive learning theory to enhance the levels of emotional understanding you can achieve from your reflections. The emotional awareness and understanding achieved through the reflective process will alert you to personal agendas that may negatively influence your ability to engage with others appropriately, but further reflection will then enable you to identify how you can adjust, modify or regulate your future responses and encourage you to plan how these changes will be achieved.

Interpersonal competence is crucial for social work practice as it ensures you can identify, acknowledge and respond appropriately to the emotions of others. Communication skills, particularly in empathic listening and empathic responses, and building relationships, are key features of this element. The reflective process again offers emotional thinking time that allows you to identify the emotions being communicated by others so that you can offer an appropriate empathic response.

While intrapersonal and interpersonal abilities are important in their own right, what is more important is that you recognize how they are closely interlinked. Your own journey to becoming emotionally self-aware increases your ability to recognize and understand the emotional responses of others, and by regulating your own emotional responses you become more attuned to others' emotions. Once you have achieved intrapersonal competence, you can focus more clearly on the development of your empathic skills and the achievement of interpersonal competence.

Having a knowledge base to inform your understanding of reflection is crucial if you are to become a competent reflective practitioner, but it is equally important that you develop an ability to apply this knowledge in practice to benefit from the reflective process and provide evidence of your reflective skills to others.

To help with this next stage, Chapter 5 alerted you to the common obstacles you may encounter in practice and offered practical solutions to help you overcome or avoid such difficulties impacting on your attempts to integrate reflective practice in your normal working routines. Factors such as time, confidence and working environments have been highlighted as potential challenges, and therefore it is vital that you plan how to use your reflective time effectively and efficiently and have a range of reflective tools available to use while you are developing your own reflective techniques.

Brockbank and McGill's (1998) 'six wisemen' questions can be applied to help you plan and prioritize your reflections, draw out your personal key issues, and help you to focus on specific future actions (Jasper, 2006). For example:

'What' questions help you select an appropriate event for your reflections – e.g. 'What areas of my practice do I need to develop?'; 'What event might enable me to focus on this area of practice?'

'Why' questions ensure you have clear purpose and goals for this reflective process – e.g. 'Why is this area of development significant for me?'

'When' questions ensure that you identify an appropriate time for your reflections – e.g. 'When would be the best time for me to undertake this reflection effectively?'

'Where' questions encourage you to consider the most productive location for your reflections – e.g. 'Where do I achieve my most productive learning?'

'Who' questions enable you to decide if others should be involved – e.g. 'Who might I involve that would enhance the outcomes of my reflections in this instance?'

'How' questions encourage you to consider what action needs to be taken to ensure your reflections produce constructive outcomes – e.g. 'How can I effectively reflect on this event?' (which tool is likely to be most effective?), or 'How might I alter my practice in the future?', 'How might I improve my knowledge of.........?'

If you do not make time for reflection, you lose the opportunity to use your experiences as a springboard for future professional development. Using these prompts allows you to create an effective reflective environment that enables you to make efficient use of the limited time that may be available to you and allows you to take responsibility for your own learning and development.

The reflective tools offered in the chapter are specifically designed to facilitate the reflective process by providing a framework, consisting of reflective questions, which prompts you to question, analyse and evaluate practice experiences. These structured activities aim to help you 'tap into' your technical knowledge, practice wisdom, skills, professional values and personal beliefs and feelings so that you can begin to understand how these components come together to create your own unique practice strengths and areas of development.

Before you can fulfil the requirements of your professional education and training you will be required to provide evidence of your ongoing progress and development as a reflective practitioner and competent professional to others. While the reflective tools offer a clear structure on which to base any written reflective accounts you might share with others, your course of study is likely to have designed a range of written reflective tasks or academic assignments which will provide opportunities for you to demonstrate the outcomes of your reflections and capture your learning and professional development.

To ensure you can create an accurate record of your growing reflective skills and professional development, Chapter 6 provided guidance on 'what' and 'how' to write reflectively from two different perspectives: free-flowing reflective accounts, for your own benefit, and purposeful reflecting writing, for accounts intended for those responsible for assessing your competence.

The true purpose and benefit of reflective writing are not associated with providing evidence of your developing skills to others, but rather to increase the depth and quality of the learning achieved from retrospectively examining practice experiences. The process of compiling a written reflective account encourages you to explore events to a new level by 'tapping into' information that lies below the surface of your consciousness, resulting in an increased awareness of the thoughts and feelings that influence your interpretation of events and enhancing the learning achieved by asking reflective questions.

Maintaining an ongoing record of your reflective conversations with yourself has been recommended so that you can write freely and document your developmental journey over time. This visual record of your current thinking, awareness, knowledge and learning not only enhances your ability to unravel the complexities involved in becoming a competent practitioner, it also provides a map of your learning and achievements that can inform self-assessments and provides material that can be adapted to fit the purposeful reflective accounts you will complete for others.

When writing purposeful reflective accounts your intention is to address the specific criteria required by each task. You should avoid descriptive writing by making use of reflective questions that critically analyse, evaluate and challenge current 'knowing' and 'doing', consider different perspectives and identify future actions. Remember to highlight your growing application of knowledge and values in practice, as well as identifying your professional challenges and concerns, to maintain a balance in these reflective accounts and demonstrate your progress and development.

To ensure that you benefit fully from your reflective accounts the chapter concluded with some practical suggestions to encourage positive habits, but your own individual advance planning is most effective when deciding on:

- How you might store and maintain your reflective accounts – written or typed entries?
- Where, when and how often you will write.

Remember to ensure that confidentiality is maintained in all records pertaining to your developmental journey.

You are now armed with sufficient technical knowledge, effective strategies, an awareness of potential challenges, and a selection of reliable tools and relevant skills to confidently move forward and directly experience the benefits of reflecting 'in' and 'on' practice.

Learning in practice is a central feature of your professional education and training as it provides invaluable opportunities for you to grow and develop your professional 'self'. By engaging in 'real-life' professional activities you gain a deeper understanding of the application of professional knowledge, skills and values, construct your professional identity, become familiar with professional and organizational cultures, develop your professional confidence and establish your commitment to ongoing personal and professional development. Reflecting 'in' and 'on' practice enables you to extract learning from these practice experiences, allowing you to improve your professional performance and achieve the necessary standard of professional competence.

Practice-based experiences involve a range of individuals who will play a part in facilitating and assessing your performance and development. To enable all participants to reap the rewards offered by these indispensable learning experiences, Chapter 7 focused attention on the creation of a positive learning environment that was conducive to learning and development, produced credible and accurate assessments of students' achievements and professional competence, and was informed by reflective practice. Achieving an environment where participants work collaboratively, address power imbalances, understand the learning process and engage in effective supervision provides a solid foundation for reflective practice to flourish and encourages and supports the learning and development of all those involved.

The chapter had an additional message to offer, going beyond reflecting on your performance with service users and carers, to consider wider professional responsibilities that include developing your ability to work collaboratively with colleagues and other professionals and actively taking responsibility for your own professional development. Achieving these professional responsibilities is equally crucial to the development of your professional competence and requires you to commit to the learning process by regularly reflecting on your approach to learning, establishing open communication with others, valuing and respecting others' contribution to your learning and monitoring and evaluating your ability to relate to colleagues and other professionals. Reflecting on this aspect of your professional 'self' allows you to identify personal barriers and take action that will enable you to value and benefit from the contribution of others, not only during your developmental journey but throughout your professional career.

You have now explored all of the components necessary to develop a good working knowledge and understanding of reflection and reflective practice and made progress towards your goal of achieving a 'questioning approach' through the reflective activities provided in the text. The level of reflective skill you achieve will develop over time, with practise, and in parallel with the development of your professional knowledge, skills and values. My final suggestion for you would be to persevere, believe in yourself, and trust in the reflective process (Bolton, 2010). Remember to look after yourself so that you can effectively care for others, enjoy the satisfaction you will achieve by recognizing your strengths as a competent practitioner, and take confidence from your motivation to continually strive to improve your practice through critical reflection.

I hope you have found the content of the book useful and that the knowledge and understanding you have achieved give you the confidence to move forward and experience the benefits of reflective practice in your ongoing journey to become a more competent and confident professional.

I wish you well in your future social work career.

Appendix 1

Contact details: Professional regulatory councils

Care Council for Wales (CCW): www.ccwales.org.uk (Wales)

General Social Care Council (GSCC): www.hcpc-uk.org (England) (abolished July 2012, replaced August 2012 by the Health and Care Professions Council (HCPC) www.hcpc-uk.org)

Northern Ireland Social Care Council (NISCC): www.niscc.info (Northern Ireland)

Scottish Social Services Council (SSSC): www.sssc.uk.com (Scotland)

Contact details: Regulatory bodies for care standards

Care Quality Commission (CQC) England: www.cqc.org.uk

Care Standards Inspectorate for Wales: www.csiw.wales.gov.uk

Scottish Commission for the Regulation of Care Scotland: www.carecommission.com

The Regulation and Quality Improvement Authority (RQIA), Northern Ireland: www.rqia.org.uk

Appendix 2

National occupational standards (incorporated in the SSSC Siswe, 2003)

Key role 1

Prepare for, and work with, individuals, families, carers, groups and communities to assess their needs and circumstances.

Key role 2

Plan, carry out, review and evaluate social work practice with individuals, families, carers, groups and communities, and other professionals.

Key role 3

Assess and manage risk to individuals, families, carers, groups, communities, self and colleagues.

Key role 4

Demonstrate professional competence in social work practice.

Key role 5

Manage and be accountable, with supervision and support, for your own social work practice within your organization.

Key role 6

Support individuals to represent and manage their needs, views and circumstances.

Sources: TOPPS (2002); CCW (2003a); NISCC (2003); SSSC (2003).

Appendix 3

Code of practice for social care workers

As a social care worker you must:

1 Protect the rights and promote the interests of service users and carers.
2 Establish and maintain the trust and confidence of service users and carers.
3 Promote the independence of service users while protecting them as far as possible from danger or harm.
4 Respect the rights of service users while seeking to ensure that their behaviour does not harm themselves or other people.
5 Uphold public trust and confidence in social care services.
6 Be accountable for the quality of your work and take responsibility for maintaining and improving your knowledge and skills.

Sources: GSCC (2002a); NISCC (2002); CCW (2003b); SSSC (2005).

References

Bandura, A. (1965) Influence of a Model's Reinforcement Contingencies on the Acquisition of Imitative Responses, *Journal of Personality and Social Psychology,* 1: 589–95.

Bandura, A. (1977) *Social Learning Theory.* Englewood Cliffs, New Jersey: Prentice Hall.

Banks, S. (2006) *Ethics and Values in Social Work,* 3rd edition. Basingstoke: Palgrave Macmillan.

Barlow, C. and Hall, B. L. (2007) What About Feelings? A study of emotion and tension in social work field education, *Social Work Education: The International Journal,* 26(4): 399–413.

Beatty, L. (2003) Supporting Student Learning from Experience, in M. Fry, S. Ketteridge and S. Marshall (eds) *A Handbook for Teaching and Learning in Higher Education: Enhancing academic practice,* 2nd edition. London: Kogan Page.

Beck, A. T. (1976) *Cognitive Therapy and the Emotional Disorders.* New York: International Universities Press.

Beckett, C. and Maynard, A. (2005) Values and Ethics in Social Work: An introduction, London: Sage: 5–23, cited in V. E. Cree (ed.) (2011) *Social Work: A Reader.* London: Routledge.

Beverley, A. and Worsley, A. (2007) *Learning and Teaching in Social Work Practice.* Basingstoke: Palgrave Macmillan.

Bolton, G. (2001) *Reflective Practice Writing and Professional Development.* London: Sage.

Bolton, G. (2010) *Reflective Practice Writing and Professional Development,* 3rd edition. London: Sage.

Borton, T. (1970) *Reach, Teach, Touch: Student concerns and process education.* New York: McGraw-Hill.

Boud, D., Keogh, R. and Walker, D. (1985) *Reflection: Turning experience into learning.* London: Kogan Page.

Boud, D. and Walker, D. (1998) Promoting Reflection in Professional Courses: The challenge of context, *Studies in Higher Education,* 23(2): 191–206.

British Association of Social Workers (BASW) (2002) *Code of Ethics for Social Work.* Birmingham: BASW.

Brockbank, A. and McGill, I. (1998) *Facilitating Reflective Learning in Higher Education.* Buckingham: The Society for Research into Higher Education (SRHE) and Open University Press.

Brockbank, A. and McGill, I. (2007) *Facilitating Reflective Learning in Higher Education,* 2nd edition. Maidenhead: Open University Press.

Brown, A. and Bourne, I. (1996) *The Social Work Supervisor.* Buckingham: Open University Press.

Brown, K. and Rutter, L. (2009) *Critical Thinking for Social Workers,* 2nd edition. Exeter: Learning Matters.

Bruce, L., Cree, V. and Gillies, B. (2005) *Learning for Effective and Ethical Practice: Comprehensive knowledge review.* Dundee: Scottish Institute for Excellence in Social Work Education – now the Institute for Research and Innovation in Social Services (IRISS).

Bruce, L. and Lishman, J. (2004) *Learning for Effective and Ethical Practice. Agency-based practice learning: A literature review.* Dundee: The Scottish Institute for Excellence in Social Work Education – now the Institute for Research and Innovation in Social Services (IRISS).

Burrage, M., Jarausch, K. and Siegrist, H. *(1990)* An Actor-Based Framework for the Study of the Professions, in M. Burrage and R. Torstendahl (eds) *Professions in Theory and History: Rethinking the study of the professions.* London: Sage, pp. 203–25.

Butler, G. (2007) Reflecting on Emotion in Social Work, in C. Knott and T. Scragg (eds) *Reflective Practice in Social Work.* Exeter: Learning Matters.

Care Council for Wales (CCW) (2003a) *The National Occupational Standards for Social Work.* Cardiff: CCW.

Care Council for Wales (CCW) (2003b) *Code of Practice for Social Care Workers.* Cardiff: CCW.

Cherniss, C. (2000) *Emotional Intelligence: What is it and why it matters.* Consortium for Research on Emotional Intelligence in Organizations. Available at: www.eiconsortium. org (Accessed on 10 October 2011).

Clifford, S. (2010) Helping People Who are Low in Mood, in A. Grant (ed.) *Cognitive Behavioural Interventions for Mental Health Practitioners.* Exeter: Learning Matters.

Constable, G. (2007) Reflection as a Catalyst for Change, in C. Knott and T. Scragg (eds) *Reflective Practice in Social Work.* Exeter: Learning Matters.

Cottrell, S. (2003) *The Study Skills Handbook.* London: Palgrave Macmillan.

Coulshed, V. and Orme, J. (2006) *Social Work Practice,* 4th edition. Basingstoke: Palgrave Macmillan.

Cousins, C. (2004) Becoming a Social Work Supervisor: A significant role in transition, *Australian Social Work,* 57(2): 175–95.

Cree, V. E. (ed.) (2003) *Becoming a Social Worker.* London: Routledge.

Cree, V. E. (2008) Social Work in Society, in M. Davies (ed.) *The Blackwell Companion to Social Work,* 3rd edition. Oxford: Blackwell Publishing.

Cree, V. E. (ed.) (2011) *Social Work: A reader.* London: Routledge.

Crisp, B. R., Green Lister, P. and Dutton, K. (2005) Integrated Assessment: New assessment methods evaluation of an innovative method of assessment-critical incident analysis. Dundee: Scottish Institute for Excellence in Social Work Education. Available at: http://www.iriss.org.uk/resources/new-assessment-methods-evaluation-innovative-method-assessment-critical-incident-analysis (Accessed on 24 January 2012).

Cust, J. (1995) Recent Cognitive Perspectives on Learning: Implications for nurse education, *Nurse Education Today,* 15: 280–90.

Dalrymple, J. and Burke, B. (2006) *Anti-Oppressive Practice: Social care and the law,* 2nd edition. Maidenhead: Open University Press.

D'Cruz, H., Gillingham, P. and Melendez, S. (2007a) Reflexivity, its Meaning and Relevance for Social Work: A critical review of the literature, *British Journal of Social Work,* 37: 73–90.

D'Cruz, H., Gillingham, P. and Melendez, S. (2007b) Reflexivity: A concept and its meaning for practitioners working with children and families, *Critical Social Work,* 8(1).

Department of Health (DH) (1998) *Modernising Social Services: Promoting independence, improving protection, raising standards.* Cm 4169, London: TSO.

Department of Health (DH) (1999) *Building for the Future.* Cm 4051, London: TSO.

Department of Health (DH) (2000) *A Quality Strategy for Social Care*. London: DH, www.doh. gov.uk/pdfs/qstrategy.pdf.

Department of Health (DH) (2002) *Requirements for Social Work Training*. London: TSO.

Dewey, J. (1933) *How We Think*. Boston: Heath & Co.

Drakeford, M. (2008) Social Work and Politics, in M. Davies (ed.) *The Blackwell Companion to Social Work*, 3rd edition. Oxford: Blackwell Publishing.

Durkin, C. and Shergill, M. (2000) A Team Approach to Practice Teaching, *Social Work Education*, 19(2): 165–74.

Egan, G. (2007) *The Skilled Helper: A problem management and opportunity development approach to helping*, 8th edition. New York: Brooks/Cole CENGAGE Learning.

Ellis, A. (1962) *Reason and Emotion in Psychotherapy*. Secaucus, New Jersey: Lyle Stuart.

Ellis, A. and Harper, R. A. (1975) *A New Guide to Rational Living*. Englewood Cliffs, New Jersey: Prentice Hall.

Eraut, M. (1994) *Developing Professional Knowledge and Competence*. London: Falmer Press.

Evans, D. (1999) *Practice Learning in the Caring Professions*. Aldershot: Ashgate.

Fook, J. (2002) *Social Work: Critical theory and practice*. London: Sage.

Fook, J. (2007a) Uncertainty: The defining characteristics of social work, cited in V. E. Cree (ed.) (2011) *Social Work: A Reader*. London: Routledge.

Fook, J. (2007b) Reflective Practice and Critical Reflection, in J. Lishman (ed.) *Handbook for Practice Learning in Social Work and Social Care*, 2nd edition. London: Jessica Kingsley Publishers.

Fook, J. (2010) *Social Work: Critical theory and practice*. London: Sage.

Fook, J. and Askeland, G. A. (2006) The 'Critical' in Critical Reflection, in S. White, J. Fook and F. Gardner (eds) *Critical Reflection in Health and Welfare*. Maidenhead: Open University Press.

Fook, J. and Askeland, G. A. (2007) Challenges of Critical Reflection: Nothing ventured, nothing gained, *Social Work Education*, 26(5): 520–33.

Forsyth Smith, M. (2010) Working Towards Consolidation of Practice: Advice from a PQ lecturer. In S. Keen, I. Gray, J. Parker, D. Glapin and K. Brown (eds) *Newly Qualified Social Workers: A handbook for practice*. Exeter: Learning Matters.

Freshwater, D. and Stickley, T. (2004) The Heart of the Art: Emotional intelligence in nurse education, *Nursing Inquiry*, 11(2): 91–8.

Gardner, F. (2009) Affirming Values: Using critical reflection to explore meaning and professional practice, *Reflective Practice*, 10(2): 179–90.

General Social Care Council (GSCC) (2002a) *Codes of Practice for Social Workers*. London: GSCC.

General Social Care Council (GSCC) (2002b) *Codes of Practice for Social Care Employers*. London: GSCC.

General Social Care Council (GSCC) (2005) *Post-qualifying Framework for Social Work Education and Training*. London: GSCC.

Ghaye, T. (2011) *Teaching and Learning Through Reflective Practice: A practical guide for positive action*, 2nd edition. London: Taylor & Francis.

Gibbs, G. (1981) *Teaching Students to Learn; A student-centred approach*. Berkshire: Open University Press.

Gibbs, G. (1988) *Learning by Doing: A guide to teaching and learning methods*. Oxford: Further Education Unit, Oxford Polytechnic.

Gilbert, M. and Evans, K. (2000) *Psychotherapy Supervision in Context: An integrative approach.* Buckingham: Open University Press.

Goleman, D. (1996) *Emotional Intelligence: Why it can matter more than IQ.* London: Bloomsbury.

Goleman, D. (1998) *Working with Emotional Intelligence.* London: Bloomsbury.

Grant, A. (ed.) (2010) *Cognitive Behavioural Interventions for Mental Health Practitioners.* Exeter: Learning Matters.

Greenwood, J. (1998) The Role of Reflection in Single and Double Loop Learning. *Journal of Advanced Nursing.* 27:1048–53.

Hardy, C. (2004) The Art of Reflection: Reflective practice in publishing education, *Art, Design and Communication in Higher Education,* 3(1): 17–31.

Hare, I. (2004) Defining Social Work for the 21st Century: The International Federation of Social Workers' Revised Definition of Social Work, *International Social Work,* 47(3): 407–24.

Hawkins, P. and Shohet, R. (2009) *Supervision in the Helping Professions,* 3rd edition. Maidenhead: Open University Press.

Hoffman-Kipp, P., Artiles, A. and Lopez-Torres, L. (2003) Beyond Reflection: Teacher learning as praxis, *Theory into Practice,* 42(3).

Holly, M. L. (1989) *Writing to Grow: Keeping a personal-professional journal.* Portsmouth, New Hampshire: Heinemann.

Holm, D. and Stephenson, S. (1994) Reflection: A student's perspective, in A. Palmer, S. Burns and C. Bulman (eds) *Reflective Practice in Nursing: The growth of the professional practitioner.* Oxford: Blackwell Scientific Publications.

Honey, P. and Mumford, A. (2000) *The Learning Style Questionnaire.* Maidenhead: Peter Honey.

Horner, N. (2004) *What Is Social Work? Contexts and perspectives.* Exeter: Learning Matters.

Horner, N. (2009) *What Is Social Work? Contexts and perspectives,* 3rd edition. Exeter: Learning Matters.

Howe. D. (2008) *The Emotionally Intelligent Social Worker.* Basingstoke: Palgrave Macmillan.

Howe, K., Henry, M. and Renshaw, K. (2009) Managing the Personal: From surviving to thriving in social work, in S. Keen, I. Gray, J. Parker, D. Galpin and K. Brown (eds) *Newly Qualified Social Workers: A handbook for practice.* Exeter: Learning Matters.

Hugman, R. (2008) The Ethical Perspective on Social Work, in M. Davies (ed.) *The Blackwell Companion to Social Work,* 3rd edition. Oxford: Blackwell.

Humphrey, C. (2011) *Becoming a Social Worker: A guide for students.* London: Sage.

Illeris, K. (2003) Towards a Contemporary and Comprehensive Theory of Learning, *International Journal of Lifelong Education,* 22(4): 8–21.

Inskipp, F. and Procto, B. (1993) *The Art, Craft and Tasks of Counselling Supervision, Part 1: Making the most of supervision.* Twickenham, Middlesex: Cascade Publications.

International Federation of Social Workers/International Association of Schools of Social Work (IFSW/IASSW) (2004) *Ethics in Social Work: A statement of principles.* Berne: IFSW. Available at: www.ifsw.org (Accessed on 28 February 2011).

Issitt, M. (1999) Toward the Development of Anti-oppressive Reflective Practice: The challenges of multi-disciplinary working, *Journal of Practice Teaching,* 2(2): 21–36.

Jasper, M. (2003) *Beginning Reflective Practice: Foundations in nursing and health care.* Cheltenham: Nelson Thornes.

Jasper, M. (2006) *Professional Development, Reflection and Decision Making*. Oxford: Blackwell Publishing.

Jones, C. (2002) Social Work and Society, in R. Adams, L. Dominelli and M. Payne (eds) *Social Work: Themes, issues and critical debates*, 2nd edition. Basingstoke: Palgrave.

Jones, S. (2009) *Critical Learning for Social Work Students*. Exeter: Learning Matters.

Jones, S. and Joss, R. (1995) Models of Professionalism, in M. Yelloly and M. Henkel (eds) *Learning and Teaching in Social Work: Towards reflective practice*. London: Jessica Kingsley Publishers.

Kadushin, A. (1992) *Supervision in Social Work*, 3rd edition. New York: Columbia University Press.

Kearney, P. (2003) *A Framework for Supporting and Assessing Practice Learning*. Position Paper 2. London: Social Care Institute for Excellence (SCIE).

Kerka, S. (1995) *The Learning Organization: Myths and realities*. Columbus, Ohio: Eric Clearing House.

Knott, C. and Scragg, T. (2007) *Reflective Practice in Social Work*. Exeter: Learning Matters.

Knowles, M. (1984) *Andragogy in Action*. San Francisco, California: Jossey-Bass.

Knowles, M. (1990) *The Adult Learner: A neglected species*, 4th edition. Houston, Texas: Gulf Publishing Co.

Kolb, D. (1984) *Experiential Learning*. Englewood Cliffs, New Jersey: Prentice Hall.

Koole, S. L., Van Dillen, L. F. and Sheppes, G. (2009) The Self-regulation of Emotion, in K. D. Vohs and R. F. Baumeister (eds) *Handbook of Self Regulation*, Volume 2. New York: Guilford Press.

LaBoskey, V. (1993) A Conceptual Framework for Reflection in Pre-service Teacher Education, in J. Calderwood and P. Gates (eds) *Conceptualising Reflection in Teacher Development*. Lewes: Falmer Press.

Lam, C. M., Wong, H. and Leung, T. T. F. (2007) An Unfinished Reflexive Journey: Social work students' reflection on their placement experiences, *British Journal of Social Work*, 37: 91–105.

Lefevre, M. (2005) Facilitating Practice Learning and Assessment: The influence of relationship, *Social Work Education*, 24(5): 565–83.

Light, G., Cox, R. and Calkins, S. (2009) *Learning and Teaching in Higher Education: The reflective professional*. London: Sage.

Lishman, J. (2009a) Personal and Professional Development, in R. Adams, L. Dominelli and M. Payne (eds) *Social Work: Themes, issues and critical debates*, 3rd edition. Basingstoke: Palgrave Macmillan.

Lishman, J. (2009b) *Communication in Social Work*, 2nd edition. Basingstoke: Palgrave Macmillan.

Lucas, B. (2002) *Power Up Your Mind: Learn faster, work smarter*. London: Nicholas Brearley.

Macaulay, C. (2000) Transfer of Learning, in V. E. Cree and C. Macaulay (eds) *Transfer of Learning in Professional and Vocational Education*. London: Routledge.

MacDonald, G. (2007) Cognitive Behavioural Social Work, in J. Lishman (ed.) *Handbook for Practice Learning in Social Work and Social Care*, 2nd edition. London: Jessica Kingsley Publishers.

Marris, P. (1974) *Loss and Change*. London: Routledge & Kegan Paul.

McIntyre, D. (1993) Theory, Theorising and Reflection in Initial Teacher Education, in *Conceptualizing Reflection in Teacher Development*. Lewes: Flamer Press.

Mezirow, J. (ed.) (1991) How Critical Reflection Triggers Transformative Learning, *in Fostering Critical Reflection in Adulthood*. San Francisco: Jossey-Bass.

Miflin, B. (2004) Adult Learning, Self-directed Learning and Problem-based learning: Deconstructing the connections, *Teaching in Higher Education*, 9(1): 43–53.

Miller, N. and Boud, D. (1996) Animating Learning from Experience, in D. Boud and N. Miller (eds) *Working with Experience: Animating learning*. London: Routledge.

Moon, J. (1999) *Reflection in Learning and Professional Development: Theory and practice*. London: Kogan Page.

Moon, J. (2004) *A Handbook of Reflective and Experiential Learning: Theory and practice*. London: RoutledgeFalmer.

Moon, J. (2006) *Learning Journals: A handbook for reflective learning and professional development*. London: RoutledgeFalmer.

Moon, J. (2007) *Critical Thinking*. London: RoutledgeFalmer.

Moon, J. (2010) *Assessment: Learning journals and logs*. UCD Teaching and Learning/ Resources. Available at www.ucd.ie/teaching (Accessed on 25 March 2012).

Morrison, T. (2007) Emotional Intelligence, Emotion and Social Work: Context, characteristics, complications and contributions, *British Journal of Social Work*, 37: 245–63.

Munro, E. (1998) *Understanding Social Work: An empirical approach*. London: Athlone Press.

Niklasson, L. (2006) Review: Ming-sum Tsui (2005) Social Work Supervision: Context and concepts, *Forum Qualitative Sozialforschung/Forum: Qualitative Social Research*, 7(3), Art. 23. Available at www.qualitative-research.net/index.php/fqs/article/view/154/337 (Accessed on 10 May 2012).

Nolan, M. and Caldock, K. (1996) Assessment: Identifying the barriers to good practice, *Health and Social Care in the Community*, 4: 77–85.

Northern Ireland Social Care Council (NISCC) (2002) *Code of Practice for Social Care Workers*. Belfast: NISCC.

Northern Ireland Social Care Council (NISCC) (2003) *The National Occupational Standards for Social Work*. Belfast: NISCC.

Overholster, J.C. (2004) The Four Pillars of Psychotherapy Supervision, *The Clinical Supervisor*, 23(1): 1–13.

Papell, C. (1996) Reflections on Issues in Social Work Education, in N. Gould and I. Taylor (eds) *Reflective Learning for Social Work*. Farnhem: Ashgate Publishing.

Parker, J. (2010) *Effective Practice Learning in Social Work*, 2nd edition. Exeter: Learning Matters.

Payne, M. (2005) *The Origins of Social Work: Continuity and change*. Basingstoke: Palgrave Macmillan.

Pearsall, J. and Hanks, P. (2003) *Oxford Dictionary of English*, 2nd edition. Oxford: Oxford University Press.

Pehrson, K. L., Panos, P. T., Larson, K. L. and Cox, S. E. (2009) Enhancement of the Social Work Field Practicum Student–Supervisor Relationship: Utilising communication styles, *Journal of Practice Teaching and Learning*, 9(2): 72–92.

Practice Learning Taskforce (2003) *Practice Learning in Focus*. Edinburgh: Department of Health.

Preston-Shoot, M. (2003) Changing Learning and Learning Change: Making a difference in education and policy and practice, *Journal of Social Work Practice*, 17: 10–23.

Polanyi, M. (1967) *The Tacit Dimension*. New York: Doubleday.

Pollard, A. and Tann, S. (1994) *Reflective Teaching in Primary Schools*, 2nd edition. London: Cassell.

Quality Assurance Agency for Higher Education (QAA) (2000) *Benchmark Statement for Social Policy and Social Work*. Gloucester: QAA.

Raelin, J. (2002) I Don't Have Time to Think! Versus The Art of Reflective Practitioner, *Reflections*, 4(1): 66–79.

Rich, A. and Parker, D. L. (1995) Reflection and Critical Incident Analysis: Ethical and moral implications of their use within nursing and midwifery education, *Journal of Advanced Nursing*, 22: 1050–7.

Ringel, S. (2001) In the Shadow of Death: Relationship paradigms in clinical supervision, *Clinical Social Work Journal*, 29(2): 171–9.

Roberts, A. (2009) Encouraging Reflective Practice in Periods of Professional Workplace Experience: The development of a conceptual model, *Reflective Practice*, 10(5): 633–44.

Rogers, J. (2001) *Adult Learning*. Buckingham: Open University Press.

Rolfe, G. (1998) *Expanding Nursing Knowledge: Understanding and researching your own practice*. Oxford: Butterworth-Heinemann.

Rolfe, G., Freshwater, D. and Jasper, M. (2001) *Critical Thinking for Nursing and the Helping Professions*. Basingstoke: Palgrave.

Ruch, G. (2000) Self and Social Work: Towards an integrated model of learning, *Journal of Social Work Practice*, 14: 99–111.

Ruch, G. (2002) From Triangle to Spiral: Reflective practice in social work education, practice and research, *Social Work Education*, 21(2): 199–216.

Ryan, M. (2011) Improving Reflective Writing in Higher Education: A social semiotic perspective, *Teaching in Higher Education*, 16: 99–111.

Schön, D. A. (1983) *The Reflective Practitioner: How professionals think in action*. London: Temple Smith.

Schön, D. A. (1987) *Educating the Reflective Practitioner: Towards a new design for teaching and learning in the professions*. San Francisco, California: Jossey-Bass.

Sciulli, D. (2005) Continental Sociology of Professions Today: Conceptual contributions, *Current Sociology*, 53(6): 915–42.

Sciulli, D. (2007) Professions Before Professionalism, *European Journal of Sociology*, 48(1): 121–47.

Scottish Executive (1998) *Modernising Social Work Services: A consultation paper on workforce regulation and education*. Edinburgh: Scottish Executive.

Scottish Executive (1999) *Aiming for Excellence: Modernising social work services in Scotland*, Cm 4288. Edinburgh: HMSO.

Scottish Executive (2005) *National Strategy for Development of the Social Service Workforce: A plan for action 2005–2010*. Edinburgh: Scottish Executive.

Scottish Executive (2006a) *Changing Lives: Report of the 21st century social work review*. Edinburgh: Scottish Executive.

Scottish Executive (2006b) *Key Capabilities in Child Care and Protection*. Edinburgh: Scottish Executive.

Scottish Social Services Council (SSSC) (2003) *The Framework for Social Work Education in Scotland*. Dundee: SSSC.

Scottish Social Services Council (SSSC) (2005) *Codes of Practice for Social Services Workers and Employers.* Dundee: SSSC.

Scottish Social Services Council (SSSC) (2008) *The Framework for Continuous Learning in Social Services.* Dundee: SSSC.

Seebohm, F. (1968) *Report of the Committee on Local Authority and Allied Social Services,* Cmnd 3703. London: HMSO.

Seidel, S. and Blythe, T. (1996) Reflective Practice in the Classroom. Unpublished article: Project Zero/Massachusetts Schools Network.

Shardlow, S. and Doel, M. (1996) *Practice Learning and Teaching.* Basingstoke: Macmillan.

Shaw, I. (1985) A Closed Profession? Recruitment to Social Work, *British Journal of Social Work,* 15: 261–80.

Sheppard, M. (2007) Assessment: From reflexivity to process knowledge, in J. Lishman (ed.) *Handbook for Practice Learning in Social Work and Social Care: Knowledge and theory,* 2nd edition. London: Jessica Kingsley Publishers.

Siegrist, H. (2002) Professionalization/Professions in History, in *International Encyclopedia of the Social and Behavioural Sciences.* Amsterdam: Elsevier Science.

Social Work Services Inspectorate (SWSI) (2004) *Confidence in Practice Learning.* Edinburgh: Scottish Executive.

Social Work Task Force (SWTF) (2009) *Building a Safe, Confident Future: The final report of the social work taskforce.* Available at http://publications.dcsf.gov.uk (Accessed on 10 November 2011).

Sparrow, J. (2009) Impact of Emotions Associated with Reflecting upon the Past, *Reflective Practice,* 10(5): 567–76.

Statham, D. (ed.) (2004) *Managing Front Line Practice in Social Care.* London: Jessica Kingsley.

Stepney, P. (2006) Mission Impossible? Critical Practice in Social Work, *British Journal of Social Work,* 36: 1289–307.

Suskie, L. (2004) *Assessing Student Learning: A common sense guide.* Boston, Massachusetts: Anker Publishing.

Taylor, B. J. (2010) *Reflective Practice for Healthcare Professionals,* 3rd edition. Maidenhead: Open University Press.

Thompson, N. (2000) *Theory and Practice in Human Services.* Maidenhead: Open University Press.

Thompson, N. (2009) *Practising Social Work.* Basingstoke: Palgrave Macmillan.

Thompson, N. and Thompson, S. (2008a) *The Social Work Companion,* Basingstoke: Palgrave Macmillan.

Thompson, N. and Thompson, S. (2008b) *The Critically Reflective Practitioner.* Basingstoke: Palgrave Macmillan.

Training Organization for the Personal Social Services (TOPPS) (2002) *The National Occupational Standards for Social Work.* Leeds: TOPPS.

Trevithick, P. (2008) Revisiting the Knowledge Base of Social Work: A framework for practice, *British Journal of Social Work,* 38: 1212–37.

Trotter, S. (1999a) Journal Writing to Promote Reflective Practice in Pre-Service Teachers. Paper presented to the International Human Science Research Conference, Sheffield, July.

Trotter, C. (1999b) *Working with Involuntary Clients: A guide to practice.* St Leonards, New South Wales: Allen and Unwin.

Tsui, M. S. (2005) *Social Work Supervision: Contexts and concepts*. Thousand Oaks, California: Sage.

Van Manen, J. (1977) Linking Ways of Knowing and Ways of Being, *Curriculum Enquiry*, 6: 205–8.

Walker, J. C. (1992) *Standards and Partnerships in Teacher and Teaching Education: USA and UK experience*. Canberra: University of Canberra, Centre for Research in Professional Education.

Walker, J., Crawford, K. and Parker, J. (2008) *Practice Education in Social Work*. Exeter: Learning Matters.

Wilkie, G. and Raffaelli, D. (2005) In at the Deep End: Making transitions from SpR to consultant, *Advances in Psychiatric Treatment*, 11: 107–14.

Yelloly, M. and Henkel, M. (eds) *Learning and Teaching in Social Work: Towards reflective practice*. London: Jessica Kingsley.

Zeichner, K. and Liston, D (1996) *Reflective Teaching: An introduction*. Mahwah, New Jersey: Lawrence Erlbaum Associates.

Index